THE
POWER
OF
FEEDBACK

THE POWER OF FEEDBACK

35 Principles
for
Turning Feedback
from Others into
Personal and Professional
Change

JOSEPH R. FOLKMAN

WILEY

JOHN WILEY & SONS, INC.

Published by John Wiley & Sons, Inc., Hoboken, New Jersey.
Published simultaneously in Canada.

For general information on our other products and services or for
technical support, please contact our Customer Care Department within
the United States at (800) 762-2974, outside the United States at (317)
572-3993 or fax (317) 572-4002.

Wiley also publishes its books in a variety of electronic formats. Some
content that appears in print may not be available in electronic books.
For more information about Wiley products, visit our web site at
www.wiley.com.

Library of Congress Cataloging-in-Publication Data:

Folkman, Joe.
   The power of feedback : 35 principles for turning feedback from
others into personal and professional change / Joseph R. Folkman.
       p.   cm.
   Includes bibliographical references and index.
   ISBN 13: 978-0-471-99820-4 (cloth)
   ISBN 10: 0-471-99820-6 (cloth)
   1. Communication in organizations.   2. Feedback (Psychology)
   3. Organizational change.   I. Title.
   HD30.3.F65   2006
   650.1'3—dc22
                                                           2006005659

Printed in the United States of America.

10 9 8 7 6 5 4 3 2 1

To my family,
who continue to give me feedback
and patiently wait for change.

Contents

Foreword

In 1798, Scottish poet Robert Burns wrote:

> "O wad some Power the giftie gie us
> To see oursels as ithers see us!
> It wad frae mony a blunder free us . . ."

Burns clearly saw the need for people to develop more accurate views of their behavior, because it would free them from committing many of life's mistakes. The solution that Burns' poem suggests, however, is for some divine Power to provide that wonderful insight. As far as I can tell, that has not been happening for the great majority of us.

I would like to believe that Burns would rejoice to learn, some 200 years later, that people are seeing the same need he saw, but they are discovering powerful and practical vehicles to make that occur, without troubling the divine, cosmic Powers to take the responsibility. Burns probably could not have envisioned the day described in the book you are about to read. He would be amazed at the practical tools that have been created to help us shrink the gap between how we're seen and how others see us.

Some books are worthy of being recommended simply because of their subject matter. Their topic is of such import that any treatise presenting new ideas and a useful way to frame the subject would be worth the investment of time and money to read. The topic of feedback fits that description. There is no greater force to improve the quality of human relationships or improve the way organizations function than to multiply the amount and improve the quality of feedback.

Other books are worthy of being recommended because their content is of great practical use, such as when an author takes an otherwise abstract, obtuse subject and turns it into an actionable, practical set of things to do. Joe Folkman has accomplished that task by presenting key findings from his long career in helping individuals and organizations to develop feedback-rich environments. He has devoted his career to the important issue of helping individuals and organizations change through the use of a variety of surveys and feedback instruments. But his message goes far beyond the creation of better instruments to address the more important issues of how such instruments are to be used and the degree to which dedicated follow-up should occur. Therein lies the truly important contribution of his book. Better yet, he presents compelling statistical evidence for what happens when these steps are taken.

Finally, some books contain information of high value, but the effort required to extract that information often exceeds the value derived. I predict that most readers will be entranced by the extensive illustrations and examples from Joe Folkman's consulting background that clarify these principles and make them come alive. Ordinarily, employee surveys and feedback tools would rival macroeconomics for sheer lack of excitement, but in this case, the author has made this topic highly engaging and accessible.

So, here you have the best of everything—an important topic; a talented, entertaining, and highly qualified author; content that is practical, and a text written in an easily comprehended manner. Enjoy.

John H. "Jack" Zenger

Acknowledgments

This book emerged as a result of the work I have done in assessing individual effectiveness over the past 30 years. Helping organizations to design, gather, and process feedback has provided an opportunity for me to see many people make significant and meaningful changes. Thousands of brave and courageous people over the years have contributed greatly to the content of this book. Their ideas, experiences, and feedback have been invaluable to me. To begin with, this book would not have been possible without the many supportive clients who provided a learning laboratory for testing and refining this change technology. To all those who worked with us and provided us with insights and new opportunities for learning: thank you.

Special thanks to Gene Dalton who wrote the Foreword to my earlier book, *Turning Feedback into Change*. Gene has since passed away, but his example and extraordinary work live on. Many of the new ideas in this book came out of research I did with John H. "Jack" Zenger presented in our recent book, *The Extraordinary*

Leader. I have truly appreciated working with Jack and acknowledge his contributions. We enjoyed working together so much, we decided to create a firm to nurture and build on our original research.

I appreciate all my colleagues at Zenger | Folkman, our current firm, where many of the ideas in this book took shape. I also appreciate many friends and colleagues who have shared their experiences and learning throughout my career, which have contributed to this book.

I also express appreciation to Trent Price, for his work in editing the manuscript and to Jenny Gildea for her work preparing the manuscript. And I gratefully acknowledge Matthew Holt and Kate Lindsay at Wiley for their enthusiasm and support of this project.

Finally, thanks to my wonderful and supportive wife, Laura, and our five children, who continue to have unwavering faith in me and my abilities.

Introduction

Feedback can be very powerful. Those who look for and accept it position themselves to be more competent and capable. Those who resist, reject, or avoid it doom themselves to the limitations of their own personal insights—which may be right or wrong, but they will never know. They fail to see the power in feedback.

Without feedback we are flying blind. Others see things we can't see. In performance assessments designed to measure individual effectiveness, it has been found that those who are the least effective at accurately predicting their strengths and weaknesses are the individuals themselves.

In an assessment looking at over 1,000 managers, we asked direct reports if their managers actively looked for opportunities to get feedback. Only 16 percent of managers had consensus from their teams that "actively looking for feedback" was a strength. Of 49 items assessing effectiveness, this item was one of the most negative. In another survey, we asked thousands of people if they regularly received feedback on their performance. Almost half of the respondents (46 percent) answered the question negatively or neutrally. Most people do not feel they lack feedback from others on how they could improve their performance at work, how they could be a better parent, how they could be a more considerate and caring spouse or friend, or simply how they could become a better person. For many people, the typical reaction to new feedback is to say, "So what, I'm too busy to do anything about it anyway."

To the question, "In the past month has someone given you feedback or made a suggestion on how you might improve?" the vast majority of us would answer, "Yes." But to the follow-up question, "Have you improved or made any changes because of that feedback?" we would likely reply, "No." Likewise, if you ask people, "Do you know of any ideas you could implement that would make you more effective?" most would reply, "Yes." But most people feel they can only juggle so many balls at a time, and so many of those ideas remain unimplemented.

Most people receive much more feedback than they are willing or able to implement. They receive feedback from many sources, including books, articles, friends, coworkers, bosses, spouses, and children. To cope with all this information, some stop listening; others become defensive. Some blame others, and others simply ignore or don't understand the feedback. The problem of receiving more feedback than we can use reminds me of an agricultural joke I was once told:

An agricultural consultant goes to visit a local farmer. After observing the operation carefully, the consultant asks the farmer if he would like some suggestions on how to improve his farm. The farmer replies, "No, I already know dozens of things I should be doing to run this farm better, and I don't do any of those. Why should I add more to the list?"

A growing trend is to provide people with more and more performance feedback on their strengths and weaknesses. Companies institute performance appraisal processes with more feedback, including upward evaluations, 360-degree or four-way feedback, and peer evaluation systems. These companies hope to involve more people than just the boss in assessing a person's performance. The idea behind the trend is the more information and feedback people receive, the more effective they will be.

Getting feedback from multiple sources is an effective way to discover the strengths and weaknesses in our performance. Feedback frequently helps us understand the attributes we would not otherwise notice, but which may be obvious to others. Although people are receiving more feedback, changes in their behavior do not seem to be taking place. As with antibiotics that are used too frequently, people quickly begin to build immunities to feedback and resist making changes.

Also, people who receive an abundance of helpful feedback early in their careers often find, later in their careers when they become managers, the feedback seems less open, honest, and straightforward, and more politically loaded. To help managers obtain more open and candid feedback, many organizations now ask employees to complete anonymous surveys for each manager at several key points: those who manage the manager, the manager's peers, and those who report to the manager. But, although the feedback process has become an increasingly popular way to "send the message," frequently the people receiving the feedback still do not "get the message," nor do they change as a result of the process.

The purpose of this book is to help you accept, prioritize, plan for, and change as a result of the feedback you receive. The approach I use has been refined through my experience in working with thousands of people who have received performance feedback. The people who change as a result of feedback are not necessarily stronger or smarter than those who don't, but by following a few simple principles and steps, lasting and effective change is possible.

WHY THIS BOOK?

As I considered writing this book, I thought about how I could provide new insights and expand on the ideas described in my first book, *Turning Feedback into Change.* Many people who read that book indicated it had been very helpful. For over 10 years, it has guided people to process and apply the feedback they receive. In fact, my personal mission during the first 20 years or so of my career—largely in the area of designing feedback systems and providing people with feedback—might best have been characterized as "helping people figure out what is wrong and then fixing it." During those years, I followed that mission diligently. In 1999, Jack Zenger and I began a detailed analysis of hundreds of thousands of feedback surveys collected over many years. Our research uncovered some powerful new insights. Our analysis led me to verify some of the advice I had been giving to clients over the years, but it also caused me to question other advice. For this reason, I felt a strong need to write a new book and share some of these amazing findings.

For most people, giving and receiving feedback has been more of a negative than a positive experience. Although most feedback results contain both positive and negative feedback, by and large most people focus on the negative and believe that the key to self-improvement is found in fixing their weaknesses. In our research, we found that the key to predicting highly effective people was not the absence of weaknesses, but rather the presence of a few profound strengths. To be perceived by others as highly effective, people need to have strengths. We also found that successful people do not have to be perfect at everything, but they do need to be highly effective at a few important skills. Feedback not only ought to help people discover what they need to do to improve, but it also ought to help them understand what skills they could develop into strengths. A key to being highly successful is doing some things well. But investing all our time and energy in fixing our weaknesses does not necessarily help us build strengths. The results of our research made it clear that developing a moderate strength into a profound strength would have a far greater impact on performance than fixing something that was slightly below average.

Change is difficult. It takes great commitment, effort, and practice. The one key ingredient that is an absolute necessity for change to occur is passion. We can't change something that others want us to change when we half-heartedly agree to "work on it." So, rather than working on fixing issues that you don't really care about, why not find an issue for which you have a passion? Too often, people feel they need to work to change issues that others want them to change. This attitude represents compliance, not commitment.

The process of going from poor performance to good performance is more straightforward than going from good to great. It is usually very clear what needs to be done to improve poor performance or to overcome "fatal flaws." Weakness, errors, or problems are easily seen and the solutions are often intuitively obvious. But the process of going from good to great is much harder. People talk about "building strengths," but in our research we learned that the process is different. The great learning from the analysis was that people who have exceptional skills in a specific area are also skillful in performing some of what we call "companion behaviors." What creates exceptional ability is the interaction of multiple skills. We also found that improvement in companion skills would have a remarkable impact on perceived performance.

Everyone seems to have some skill or ability that might be thought of as a gift or strength. We seem to gravitate toward that activity whenever we have a choice. Our continual approach of accepting our gifts but working to improve our weakness has many of us trying to change things we don't care much about, but we dutifully go about trying to do it anyway. In a series of recent seminars, I asked people to write down the one skill that, if they performed it with a high level of expertise, would make the most difference in their ability to be successful in their current job. It was not difficult for people to identify this skill. After they had written down the skill that came to mind, I then asked them to review performance objectives that had been established with their managers six months before. Only about 20 percent of the people were working on improving the one skill that would help them the most. This book explores the process of moving from fixing weaknesses to building on strengths.

When I was a teenager, I attended a party in which someone demonstrated a magic trick called "broom over." Everyone was seated in a circle, and a person in the center of the circle held a broom. Another person would walk into a closet, where he or she could hear, but not see what was going on. The person in the center of the circle would hold the broom over the head of someone sitting in the circle and say, "Broom over, broom over who?" Then the person in the middle would sit back down in the center of the circle, and the person waiting in the closet would come out and guess the person who'd had the broom held over his or her head. The person holding the broom and the person in the closet were 100 percent accurate.

We tried to figure out how the trick worked. We came up with some very complicated ways of prediction, such as, "It's every fourth person to the right, switching from girl to boy each time." It took a long time for us to figure out how the trick worked, but in the end the process was simple. The last person to laugh was it. The subtle difficulty of the game was that those in the circle determined the next person who would have the broom overhead. Such magic tricks look complicated, but in the end they are always very simple. Most people fail to see the subtlety of how the trick works.

Trying to figure out how to be successful in life is very similar to watching this magic trick. Things often look very complicated. People try to think up very complex explanations. But, in my experience, feedback is one of those very simple explanations to help us understand a complex mystery. It seems so simple that many fail to see the power of feedback.

It is my hope that sharing these new insights with you and placing them in context will give you many more powerful tools in your efforts to discover the power of feedback.

1

Reacting to Feedback

The process of giving thousands of people feedback on their individual performance has uncovered several clear and defined principles of feedback that generally apply in most interactions involving feedback. We begin by discussing each of those principles.

PRINCIPLE 1

Asking others for input increases their expectation that you will change in a positive way.

Many who receive feedback turn that feedback into measurable change. However, others receiving feedback do not change. This frustrates not only those receiving the feedback, but also those providing the feedback. This leads to a second principle.

PRINCIPLE 2

*If you receive feedback but do not change for the bet-
ter, you will be perceived more negatively than if you
had not received feedback.*

You can compound your negative feedback by ignoring
or rejecting it. When people receive feedback, they
react. Their reactions may range from extremely negative to extremely positive, or there may be no visible
reaction at all. Regardless of the reaction, a third principle emerges.

PRINCIPLE 3

*You will not change what you do not believe needs
to be changed.*

A personal feedback experience is fundamentally different from looking at a production report or an accounting
statement. Even though someone may provide feedback
in a way that leaves no room for doubt or difficulty in
understanding, this does not necessarily guarantee that
people will believe the feedback, or that they will act on
it. Those who receive feedback and then make changes
or adjustments in their behavior become better people
because of the feedback. But there may be a few obsta-
cles along the way including denial.

PRINCIPLE 4

Rather than accept criticism, we tend to denounce not only what is said, but those who say it.

As people move from childhood to adulthood, the maturation process makes us more effective as adults than we were as children. However, because children have not had years of practice in denial, most of them are much more effective at accepting feedback than adults. The extent to which you have developed your denial skills determines the extent to which you accept feedback or question its accuracy.

Denial

To protect ourselves, each of us has developed a useful skill called denial. When we were children and our friends or siblings teased us, we developed the ability to say to ourselves, "They're wrong! I'm not like that."

When you receive feedback from others, if you are like most people, you will pass through some level of denial. If you feel your feedback does not point out any specific areas of change, you may be right, or you may be denying or ignoring some of the data. Likewise, if you think the feedback does not accurately reflect your true performance, again you may be right, or the feedback may be so threatening that you simply rationalize it away.

Minimal denial presents itself as rationalization. At this level, when people receive negative feedback, they either rationalize that it is not important to change, or perhaps they believe things are "not so bad." People in minimal denial are generally more aware of their rationalizations, and often can be persuaded to accept the feedback.

Moderate denial is less conscious. In this situation, people react to feedback, but they usually do not know why they are reacting. Typically, people in moderate denial display either more emotion or almost no emotion. Some people in moderate denial confront those who provided negative feedback. Others have no emotional reaction to negative feedback, and try to minimize its importance.

Those who experience *advanced denial* are not at all conscious that they are in denial. They may act as experts and assertively deny that a problem exists, or they may totally ignore the problem. The difference is they are not consciously aware of their denial.

One key to understanding the feedback you receive is to work through your denial, and accept that the perceptions of others are, in fact, reality.

PRINCIPLE 5

All perceptions are real, at least to those who own them.

Experience suggests that the most productive approach to handle feedback is to assume they are real.

After reviewing his feedback on how well he gives instructions, and discovering the very low ratings given him by his direct reports, Steve commented, "They're wrong; I give great instructions. Those guys are just too dense to understand. The problem is not with my instructions; it's with the audience I give them to."

Steve believed that his perceptions were real and others' perceptions were wrong. Steve may be effective at giving instructions to highly trained personnel, but if his job requires that his direct reports understand his instructions, and if his instructions confuse those people, then he is not effective at giving instructions. Therefore, the perceptions of the people he manages are real.

Even when perceptions are completely inaccurate, they still represent reality. The following vignette illustrates this point:

Suppose I were to build a structurally sound and safe bridge that adheres to all laws and principles of engineering. But, because of the unique design of the bridge, most people perceive that my bridge is not safe or structurally sound.

Although it is clear to me that those perceptions are not true, to the people who believe the bridge is unsafe, their perceptions are real. If the bridge was built to help people cross a river, but people think the bridge is unsafe and therefore do not use the bridge, of what value would the bridge be?

Balance

When receiving feedback, some reactive behaviors are counterproductive. However, productive behaviors are not always the simple opposites of counterproductive behaviors. For example, one counterproductive behavior is rationalization. When people over rationalize the feedback they receive, they convince themselves that nothing is wrong. They discount the feedback or even reject it outright. Such actions are counterproductive. However, the opposite behavior, taking the feedback too literally, is also counterproductive. For example, some recipients accept feedback at face value without considering reasons why the feedback could be wrong, or they read more into the feedback than was originally intended.

PRINCIPLE 6

Balancing your normal but counterproductive reactions to feedback is essential in effectively dealing with feedback.

Balance is the key to effectively dealing with feedback. For example, you must be able to balance between rationalization and taking feedback too literally. Effectively dealing with feedback may require some rationalization, but it may also require you to take some results at face value.

Those who deal most effectively with feedback are those who maintain a proper balance between counterproductive behaviors. For most people, such balance is difficult to achieve. Most people want to be told to do one thing and not another, but balance requires that we do a little of one and a little of the other, and not carry any one behavior to an extreme.

The following are four extremes or common coping strategies used in processing feedback that require balance:

1. Rationalization versus literal acceptance
2. Fight versus flight
3. "That's interesting" versus "that's terrible"
4. Paralysis of analysis versus ignorance is bliss

Rationalization versus Literal Acceptance. When people rationalize the results of their feedback, they often are trying to justify their own behavior while avoiding the underlying sources of the problem. To accept feedback from others, you must balance rationalization with taking feedback too literally.

Jill's feedback described her as an ineffective listener. When asked about the results, Jill said, "I know some of my associates don't think I listen to them, but they're wrong. I do listen. I just don't show them how well I listen. Besides, in some positions, managers have to pay a lot of attention to the people who report to them, and hold their hands. But my job isn't like that, and my people don't need it. I listen to others the same way my boss listens to me."

Jill rationalized her feedback. Some people have great rationalizing skills. Rationalizing typically involves making excuses, justifying behavior, or discrediting the feedback, and is a counterproductive behavior. We often respond to rationalization by encouraging people to accept their feedback at face value. However, some managers avoid having to think too deeply by accepting the results of their feedback surveys too literally.

As he reviewed his feedback, John showed the facilitator that his boss had rated him very highly in technical competence, but his peers and those who reported to him had rated him well below average in the same area. John had rated himself highly in technical competence. He asked the facilitator, "Who is right?"

The facilitator replied, "Both are right."

In frustration John responded, "No, I'm either technically competent or incompetent. I can't be both."

People don't always completely agree on the meaning of feedback results, because we all respond differently to the same experiences. For example, how many times have you gone to a movie with a friend and, walking away, remarked how great it was, only to have your friend remark that he or she had not liked it at all?

To accept feedback, we frequently need to balance what some people say against the differing opinions of others. John accepted the feedback from his peers and those who reported from him once he realized that his boss's criteria for technical competence differed from theirs.

Fight versus Flight. Another common strategy for dealing with feedback is to fight. To accept feedback from others, you must balance the reaction to fight against feedback with the desire to run away from it.

In response to her feedback, Jennifer told the facilitator: "I think you gave me another person's feedback. It's a simple error; I know how easily it can happen."

The facilitator told her the feedback had been checked and verified, but Jennifer still did not believe it. She reviewed the written comments to see if they applied to the situations in her department. And although she agreed that some of the written comments were about her, others did not sound right.

Over the next four days, the facilitator called the office six times, generated a computerized listing of all the results, and even calculated scores by hand to verify that it had been, in fact, Jennifer's feedback. But, despite every new piece of evidence, Jennifer looked for other problems. After four days of evidence, phone calls, and computer printouts, Jennifer finally concluded that she had given the surveys to the wrong people.

Jennifer's reaction to her feedback was to fight. Her rejection of the feedback prevented her from having to change, but it also kept her from improving. The issues she faced didn't go away just because she refused to listen. Her case is similar to a case study used in many introductory psychology classes:[1]

A patient in a mental institution believed he was dead. The therapist assigned to the patient spent one hour every day talking about what dead people do that is different from people who are alive.

The therapist asked, "Can dead people talk?"

"Yes, dead people can talk," replied the patient.

The therapist reviewed the patient's every behavior, thought process, and physical characteristic until finally, after weeks of therapy, he asked the patient, "Do dead people bleed?"

"No," replied the patient, "dead people don't bleed."

The therapist became ecstatic. He was sure he had finally found the cure. He grabbed the patient's hand, pricked it with a small pin, and watched the patient's reaction. As the patient watched the blood ooze from his finger, he looked astonished.

Looking up at the therapist, the patient exclaimed, "Gee, I guess I was wrong. Dead people *do* bleed."

Although fighting feedback or trying to prove it wrong may be counterproductive, the other extreme, "flight," can also be counterproductive. People who engage in flight or escape behavior often believe that negative feedback is more negative than actually reported. One manager reviewed her results and commented, "I always knew I was bad; this simply confirms it." While people in fight mode tend to disagree with their surveys, those in flight mode often hide from, ignore, or allow themselves to be destroyed by the results. This tactic allows them to avoid correcting the problem by escaping from it.

Why is the process of receiving feedback so threatening? Most people spend an exorbitant amount of time and energy trying to hide any evidence of incompetence. This is one of the reasons people go to school, get degrees, become supervisors, seek impressive titles, and hang plaques on their walls. However, we all retain some level of incompetence in many life areas. Most people have a few fears tucked away in the back of their minds about what could happen if others knew they were not competent.

Ellen's mood changed from enthusiastic and bubbly to gloomy when she received her feedback. Each page of the survey felt like a knife stabbing into her back. As Ellen read through the written comments, she shook her head in disbelief.

As the day ended, the facilitator pulled Ellen aside and asked her to stay and talk for a few minutes. As soon as everyone had left the room, the facilitator asked, "So Ellen, how is it going?"

That was all it took to release the torrents of tears she had been saving up for almost three hours. Ellen showed her report to the facilitator. Although she found herself above the norm in most areas, she had been below the norm in several others. Written comments pointed out weaknesses: "Ellen never really lets me know where I stand. She always tells me I'm doing fine, but I don't really believe her, because she tells everybody that."

Ellen had described herself as a very positive person. She felt that since taking over the group she had won the friendship of most of the employees in the group, and that they had become her friends. But how could they have done this to her? How could they have said such negative things if they were friends?

Ellen's data actually had been much more positive than that of several others in the class, and nothing in her survey's written comments had been extremely negative. The next day, several other participants shared their results with her. After seeing how negative people could be, Ellen came to realize that the results of her survey had been quite good. At that point, she began to acknowledge some of the criticism without feeling as if she had been stabbed in the back.

"That's Interesting" versus "That's Terrible." Although some people believe receiving negative feedback means the end of the world, other people read their results as if the data were an unrelated technical report. To accept feedback from others, you must balance underreaction with overreaction to feedback.

Because many of us have a bias toward rational, unemotional, and logical analysis, many people develop a "that's interesting" view toward their feedback. One engineer who had received extremely negative data remarked, "These are very interesting results, and I'm going to study them until I understand them fully."

Cigarette smoking is a useful analogy. Most people who smoke understand that smoking is hazardous to their health, and many smokers know they ought to quit. But, even though people know smoking is not good for them, and they would like to quit, many never do because they do not have a large enough "felt need."

One man, after attempting to quit smoking several times, finally succeeded. He said, "I was able to quit when I wanted to quit more than I wanted to smoke." He quit when he had a large enough "felt need" to change.

The other side of "that's interesting" is similar to the flight mentality. In the "that's terrible" mind-set, participants react as if they are shattered by each negative response in the survey. People who don't feel a strong need to change, but who continue to get negative feedback, often begin to make plans to find another position in the company or to move to another company. They will do anything rather than discuss the results and consider appropriate changes.

Paralysis of Analysis versus Ignorance Is Bliss. To accept feedback from others, you must analyze the results well enough to understand the data and its implications, without getting so caught up in the analysis that you never reach any conclusions.

Kathy, a nuclear physicist, began to analyze her data when it came back on Monday morning. By Friday, she had compiled two pages of notes for each page of results. Instead of summarizing the results, Kathy actually generated more results than she started with. She stated several times that she intended to further analyze the data "at a later time."

By the time Kathy returned to her regular duties, several pressing issues required her immediate attention, and she had to set aside her continuing analysis of the data for a while. She never did formulate any solid conclusions about her survey, even though she had put more work into its analysis than any other participant.

Contrast Kathy's paralyzing reaction to feedback with Rand's:

Rand heard the assignment clearly: "Find at least three areas that need improvement and list them in the action planning booklet."

Rand breezed through the numeric data and written comments and found what he was looking for—the most negative items. He quickly read the first three items, transferred them word for word into his booklet, and put down his pen. He raised his hand and said, "I'm done. What now?"

Rand might have also considered the following questions: "Am I sure these are the most important issues?" "How do these issues correlate with the written comments?" "Will changes in these areas have the greatest impact on how I am perceived as a manager?" And, perhaps he should have considered the fourth most negative item. It read: "Fails to make decisions based on the best available data."

When you receive feedback, you must be willing to dig in and consider the facts without getting bogged down in their analysis.

A Healthy Attitude about Feedback

If perceptions are reality, and striking an appropriate balance is important, what is the most effective way to process feedback? One way is to improve your attitude toward receiving feedback.

Situations in which no feedback is given can be frustrating. Even negative feedback helps us know where we stand, and it often contains some suggestions for improvement. Imagine how you would feel after putting a lot of effort into studying a subject for an extended period of time, taking a test on the material, and then never being allowed to find out how well you performed on the test. You would never be able to learn or improve.

A bad situation is one in which no feedback is available, or when it's only available in the form of getting terminated. Fortunately, most situations, even the most frustrating ones, do not fit this definition. Feedback typically abounds in any situation, but our reaction to the feedback often clouds our thinking and discourages other people from offering the feedback. We should perceive feedback as a welcome opportunity, not a dreaded obligation. Having an appropriate attitude toward feedback can be extremely beneficial.

PRINCIPLE 7

The process of change begins with accepting the feedback given.

Consider the following helpful ideas about how to look at feedback:

- ⊡ I enjoy feedback. I constantly look for ways to receive feedback, because of the learning opportunities offered.
- ⊡ I know feedback is difficult to give, and it is often uncomfortable for others to provide. Attacking those who provide feedback only prevents me from getting more feedback in the future. I let others know their

input is valuable. I appreciate the fact that other people took the time, effort, and personal risk to provide feedback, even if I do not agree with it.

- I would rather receive negative feedback than no feedback at all.
- Feedback can be both positive and negative, but I first consider the positive to reinforce the things I do well. I avoid dwelling on the negative and expecting the worst.
- The only people who are truly incompetent are those who refuse to listen to and accept feedback from others. No one is perfect, but those who come closest are those who continually try to improve based on the feedback they receive from others.
- Receiving negative feedback does not mean I am the worst person that ever lived. It only means that someone cares enough to tell me how to improve. If we really dislike someone, the last thing we would do is tell them how to improve.
- I believe I can change and improve. Others expect me to do something in response to their feedback, and I will find at least one thing I can do something about. I will make changes and then report to those who provided the feedback about the things I have chosen not to change and the areas I would like to change.

To improve your ability to accept feedback, it is helpful to first understand how others form impressions of you. Understanding this process should help you to balance your reactions to feedback.

2

Why Did I Get That Feedback?

How do others form impressions of us, and how do we form impressions of ourselves and our performance?

PRINCIPLE 8

Others see us differently than we see ourselves.

My history professor used to say that those who do not understand history are doomed to repeat it. I feel the same way about how people form impressions and make attributions about behavior. Understanding this process helps us answer the question, "Why do others think of me that way?" Understanding how impression formation and attribution work also helps us make the process work for us instead of against us.

The perceptions others have about us are real. People cannot be talked out of their impressions. Those impressions are created from what they observe and experience.

PRINCIPLE 9

To change the impression another person has of you, you must change your behavior.

Sometimes the impressions others have of us, though real to them, are not absolutely accurate. The focus is not on attacking them for their inaccuracy—since we can't talk them out of their impressions—but on working on ourselves. By understanding and working with the attribution process, we can create for others a more accurate perception.

Forming Impressions

It is amazing how quickly we form impressions of others. Based on very limited information, we might conclude, "This person is honest and can be trusted," or, "This person is dishonest and cannot be trusted." Recently published studies show that people make judgments in the first seconds after encountering someone. Modifying those impressions is extremely difficult.

How do you form your impressions of others? Do you use a rational approach, as if you were solving a math problem? Do you take all their traits and add them up to form overall impressions?

The process of forming impressions and making attributions about others has been extensively researched. Solomon Asch researched this question and examined two different hypotheses.[1] The first hypothesis is that we consider traits individually, and then formulate an overall impression. The following equation demonstrates this additive approach:

Overall impression = Trait A + Trait B + Trait C + Trait D

The second hypothesis is that we consider the interaction of all traits to form an overall impression. To demonstrate this, we could put drops of several different colors of food coloring into water. We do not see the individual colors for very long because they blend with the other colors. The overall impression we receive comes as a result of the blend of colors that we see.

Our overall impression tends to bias our focus on individual traits. If our overall impression of a person is positive, then we have a tendency to overlook some faults. Similarly, if our overall impression is negative, we tend to overlook the positive traits (see Figure 2.1).

After testing and considering the two hypotheses, Asch found that, rather than look at individual traits, we see the interaction of traits and form an overall impression of the entire person. We see others as a total package and do not usually focus on individual parts. Instead of seeing distinct characteristics independently from each other, we see each person as a complete whole.

Charlie had received some very negative feedback. After reviewing feedback received from his boss, peers, and those who report to him, he could see his ratings had fallen well below the norm on almost every issue. He asked, "Why don't people see some of the good things I do?"

Why Did I Get That Feedback?

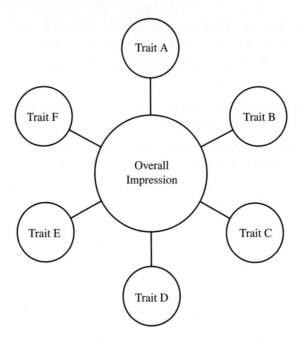

Figure 2.1   Traits interact to form an overall impression.

Even in some areas where Charlie objectively saw his performance as better than others in the work group, his ratings remained substantially worse.

Charlie's experience follows closely with what Solomon Asch found: People do not objectively judge individual issues; they bundle them collectively. People tend to rationalize individual characteristics to conform to their collective judgment. Most people would have a difficult time reconciling an overall negative impression of a person with outstanding performance in certain areas. Instead, they attribute lower performance in all areas, even though some actually may be inaccurate, to make sense of their overall impression.

Inconsistencies in performance (such as doing well at some things but poorly at others) cause us to search for sensible ways to rationalize inconsistencies. Either we change our overall impression of the person, or we ignore performance on some traits to maintain our overall impression. The reality is that ignoring some traits is easier than changing an overall impression.

However, Asch also determined that some traits have a greater influence on our overall impression than others. For example, we may acknowledge someone's weaknesses in a key area but rationalize them because we like the person and the person has strengths in other areas. But, if those weaknesses are found in critical areas, they may have a significant influence on our overall impression.

Packaging

As we observe the behavior and performance of others, we tend to "package" the information we receive. Think of the process as similar to having some large bundles of traits, attributes, and behaviors. After observing someone for a period of time, we form an overall impression.

Most people have a "library" of favorite words they use to describe different people. After some observation, we select one stereotype and assign it to a person. Many of the traits, attributes, and behaviors fit the type, but others do not. But, because we tend to hold the bundle together, we do not closely scrutinize the attributes that do not fit. For example, suppose you know a person who is very intelligent. You might also assume the person is well read. Although you can probably think of many intelligent people who do not read at all, because you have bundled "intelligent" and "well read," you assume that all intelligent people are well read. Such packaging of stereotypical traits can alter our bias toward a person either positively or negatively.

You may observe in receiving feedback from others that people may perceive and attribute positive or negative traits to you that you do not believe you actually have.

As Jean read her feedback survey, she chuckled.

"What is so amusing?" asked the facilitator.

"This feedback," she replied. "It says people feel that I am very technically competent. I'm okay technically, but not this good." She revealed that her self-analysis of technical ability indicated a very low score. "It's an area I think I need to improve, because I transferred to this section six months ago, and they do things very differently here."

"Why the positive feedback from others?" inquired the facilitator.

"Because I was good technically in my last job," she conjectured. "I think my reputation has preceded me."

The Halo Effect
The "halo effect" refers to the way our perceptions may be altered, either positively or negatively, because of our overall impressions. For example, we tend to perceive other people as physically attractive if we like them for

other reasons. Charles Dailey, in a study on jumping to conclusions, summarized the research on forming impression and bundling traits in the next principle.[2]

PRINCIPLE 10

Once people form an impression, they are not as open to information that contradicts the original impression.

Our perceptions are also heavily influenced by position, status, roles, and responsibilities. We have expectations of how people ought to perform, and we tend to judge them based on those expectations, frequently ignoring the specifics of the situation.

In research conducted at Ohio State University by Alvin Scodel and Paul Mussen, people who were considered highly authoritarian tended to rate low-authoritarian people as about as authoritarian as themselves. People low in authoritarianism rated high authoritarians as much more authoritarian than themselves. Research on dogmatism, sociability, and liberal-conservative ratings also confirm that the characteristics of the raters have a significant effect on the rating.[3]

PRINCIPLE 11

When we provide feedback, we tend to base our perceptions on our own performance and personality.

This should not come as a big surprise. Most of us are aware that our supervisors, peers, and direct reports

Why Did I Get That Feedback?

tend to like the people who act and think the same way as they do.

Explaining Others' Behavior

Suppose you saw a person kick a dog. If you were asked to explain why the person kicked the dog, your explanation would typically involve one of two approaches. One approach would be to explain the person's attitude toward the dog: "This person is very mean and hates dogs." Another approach would be to explain the environment or situation surrounding the event: "The dog tried to bite him."

Harold Kelley of UCLA describes four techniques people use to judge whether a behavior should be attributed to the person or to the environment:[4]

1 *Is the behavior distinctive?* Does this behavior occur separate from other behaviors? Is it unique? If we do not see the behavior as distinctive, we do not tend to attribute the behavior to a unique situation. For example, if I have never observed a particular person become angry, except for in one very stressful situation, then I might assume that the anger was triggered by the situation. Alternately, if I have observed or have heard that the person becomes angry often, and then I observe the person become angry in a particular situation (even if it happens to be a stressful one), I might believe that the person "always gets angry."

2 *Is the behavior consistent over time?* Anyone can achieve top performance or fail once or twice. One explanation for such performance is situational, or "luck." However, if the

THE POWER OF FEEDBACK

same performance occurs consistently, we often attribute the behavior to the person.

3 *Is the behavior consistent over situations?* Does the person maintain this same behavior in a variety of different situations? If a person performs well in one assignment but fails in another, the failure in the second assignment tends to cancel out any success in the first assignment.

4 *Is there consensus?* Is a person's behavior similar to others who are known to have these qualities? Do others I know agree with me on this person's behavior? We tend to make comparisons before we make judgments.

As people judge your behavior, they use criteria similar to these to determine whether what you do is a function of your skill (or lack of it), or the situation.

One fascinating aspect of attribution is that people typically attribute their own failure to factors in the environment. For example: "I failed because they made that job too difficult," or, "I failed because I had bad luck." But, we tend to attribute other people's success or failure to the people themselves. For example, "he failed because he did not try hard enough," or, "she failed because she just did not know how to do that job."

PRINCIPLE 12

We tend to perceive the reasons for our own failure as having to do with the situation, but we see failure in others as having to do with their effort, ability, knowledge, or character.

In an article on attribution theory, Camille Wortman notes that when bad things happen to people (disaster or tragedy), we tend to attribute the cause to the person rather than the situation.[5] For example, if a person gets mugged, we tend to say, "That person should have known better than to be on that street at night." We want to believe the place where we live is safe. If we attribute the mugging to the environment, then we must consider that we are also unsafe. Rather than live with the belief that we may encounter the same problem, we tend to attribute the cause of the problem to the people affected by the problem.

In another example, after a company layoff, employees may say, "We got rid of all the dead wood so we can be more productive." It is more threatening for employees to believe that good, competent workers were laid off than to believe the workers were unproductive and incompetent.

In an article on how we tend to react to victims, Melvin Lerner indicates that people want to believe in a just world. They want to believe that bad things happen to bad people, and good things happen to good people.[6] Many people confront this attribution process when they receive negative feedback.

When Julie reviewed her feedback survey, she became very silent. She stayed after the session to talk: "I don't know what I am going to do. It is obvious from this feedback that I will need to look for a new job."

The facilitator asked to see her survey, expecting to see something terrible. But, although the feedback pointed out some clear problems, it was not all negative. Nevertheless, the feedback had convinced Julie. She had moved beyond the simple situational explanation to the point that she believed herself to be totally and personally responsible.

Taking responsibility for feedback is generally good, but Julie believed that bad things only happened to bad people. Whenever she received bad feedback, she believed it meant that she was bad. However, good things and bad things happen to everybody. Yet, we tend to blame the individual, rather than look objectively at the situation.

Managing the Attribution Process

When people begin to understand the attribution process, they may begin to conclude that their feedback is not correct. They think that rather than being the "truth," their feedback is riddled with attributions, packaged impressions, and halo effects. But such conclusions are misleading.

PRINCIPLE 13

The feedback we receive reflects how others really feel about us and our performance.

The attribution process helps to explain how people arrive at their feelings and conclusions, but it doesn't explain them away. You may say your feedback is unfair because it does not accurately reflect your true strengths. But, as you understand more about the attribution process, you learn that the process has as much potential to work for you as it does to work against you. The better you understand the attribution process, the more you can make it work to your advantage. The attribution process is as follows:

1. *Once people form their first impressions of you, they strongly resist changing those impressions.* They vigorously defend their first impressions. And getting them to change those impressions is like causing an argument with themselves. To change those first impressions, you need some convincing arguments. One way to persuade people to change their first impression of you is to ask for their feedback and their help in making a change. Find out which attributes they pay most attention to, and the ones they seem to ignore.

2. *People form general impressions about you and then rationalize your specific characteristics and behaviors to fit those impressions.* Making small changes to any one characteristic may not be enough to change a person's overall impression of you, especially when other behaviors continue to reinforce their overall impression.

When people receive highly negative feedback, incremental improvement on a few issues frequently does not impact the overall impression. People with highly negative feedback need to consider, "What can I do to change the overall impression others have of me?" This kind of change is referred to as frame-breaking change (see Figure 2.2).

3. *People do not give equal attention to all attributes.* Some characteristics count more than others. Under-

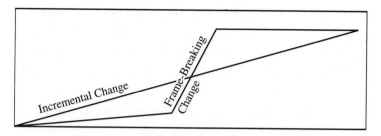

Figure 2.2   Incremental versus frame-breaking change.

standing which characteristics are most critical is an essential element in bringing about change.

4 *Small changes in specific areas can have a significant impact on others' perceptions of you and create a halo effect.* Life is not fair, and neither is what others pay the most attention to. Understanding how positive impressions are formed can be a critical element in your quest to help others see you as you really are.

5 *We tend to blame our own failures on factors in the environment, but we tend to blame the failures of others on the individual.* We might say, "I was having a bad day," or, "The situation changed" about our own situation. But we might also say, "He's just not competent to do that job," about another person's situation. The reality is that both factors—the individual and the situation—usually have at least some influence. Because others tend to blame our failures on us rather than on circumstances, we need to inform others of any adverse circumstances when we feel that our failures are influenced by the situation instead of our abilities.

Vern was a good engineer, but (as he put it), "I don't believe in beating my own drum. People should be able to figure out what I've done right and wrong without my having to explain all the details." Although Vern's attitude was noble, it directly influenced the perceptions others had about his effectiveness.

Vern had received some very negative feedback, which he felt was unfair. He later described a recent project in which he had encountered some difficult problems. He explained, "I suppose they blame all of the problems of this project on me." But Vern had never informed his boss or peers of the difficulties he'd faced with one of the suppliers, or of the fact that his client had made several late changes to the plans. Instead, Vern had learned, "In the absence of any other information, people will blame a failure on you."

[6] *Your associates do not want to believe that the source of your problems is the environment.* When an adverse circumstance causes failure, you need to provide accurate, physical evidence about the specifics of what happened, and why those specific circumstances caused you to fail.

A friend of mine, whenever he had to recount his most recent failure, would always begin by saying, "You probably won't believe this." He understood that he was stating a reality: that people are always going to be skeptical when we blame our failures on adverse circumstances. One reason for providing evidence is that, even though it may be true to you, it sounds like an excuse to them. If the "situation" could be the cause of all problems, then this world would be a very unsafe and unpredictable place, and that is not a comfortable thought.

One of the best ways to help others understand the impact of your situation is to have them pass through the experience with you. Keep in mind that your natural tendency is to blame failure on the situation, rather than to equally and objectively evaluate both your behavior and the circumstances. Obtaining situational feedback from others helps to balance your attributions.

3

Improving Your Ability to Accept Feedback

If you are having difficulty accepting feedback from others, or if you just want to improve your ability to accept feedback, how do you go about improving and making desired changes? For most people, the answer to that question sounds something like, "I would make up my mind, set a goal, become determined, and work very hard to change." Although having passion and energy is a great start, and being determined is certainly going to be important in making lasting changes, sometimes these are not enough. Using such a head-on, direct approach may help us change a little bit, but we often don't get the kinds of changes we really want.

Companion Behaviors

In recent years, I have been interested in trying to understand how people develop a high level of competence at a particular skill or ability. Research reveals that people who become highly competent at performing a certain skill also become competent at several companion skills.[1]

PRINCIPLE 14

One way of improving a skill is to improve your performance in companion skills.

After detailed research analysis, it became apparent to me that the same companion skills appear consistently in repeated studies, and companion behaviors were found to be associated with every skill studied. This breakthrough indicated that the head-on approach is only one way, and perhaps not always the best way to address the problem of change. The combination of the two skills—the desired one and a companion one—increases effectiveness and is often easier to carry out. For example, consider how an ice skater might use a combination of skills to increase effectiveness. A great ice skater can jump into the air and land gracefully on the ice. Coordination is certainly a critical skill for the skater. But, performing a jump that rises only two inches off the ice is not going to be very thrilling. So, consider a companion skill, such as strength. A triple axle is very thrilling and requires great strength, but it's only thrilling if the skater doesn't fall while landing the jump. The combination of coordination and strength is what makes the skater effective.

In our research, we looked at people who were highly effective in a specific behavior. Detailed analysis showed that people who were most effective in performing Behavior A also rated highly in several companion behaviors (Behaviors B, C, D, E, and F). Similarly, people who rated poorly in performing Behavior A also rated poorly in the same companion behaviors. It became clear that improving performance in companion behaviors might facilitate improvement in the specific behavior.

To uncover the companion behaviors associated with accepting feedback, we reviewed data from thousands of people who were receiving feedback from executives, managers, peers, direct reports, and others. In the analysis, seven companion behaviors were found that were strongly associated with accepting feedback. The seven companion skills are:

1. Integrity and honesty
2. Shows consideration and concern for others
3. Values differences
4. Develops others
5. Optimism
6. Demonstrates willingness to set stretch goals
7. Listens

These companion behaviors provide valuable insight into how you might improve your ability to accept feedback by improving your performance in companion behaviors. As you review these companion behaviors, look for the one or two behaviors that might help you in your current situation.

Integrity and Honesty. People who are effective at accepting feedback also rate highly on their integrity and honesty. Those who rate highly on integrity and honesty are described as:

- ⊡ Honest in their dealings with others
- ⊡ Consistent between their words and actions
- ⊡ Walks the talk
- ⊡ Trusted

People who are honest and straightforward with others tend to be honest and straightforward about themselves, but those who shade the truth (even slightly) with others have the same tendency to shade the truth about themselves. Those who deceive others tend to deceive themselves as well. They not only lie to themselves, but they soon believe their own lies. In fact, I don't believe that people can be honest with themselves and dishonest with others. In this case, the path to improvement starts with being honest, direct, and straightforward with others.

Many may think integrity and honesty only applies to convicted criminals, and that these are the only truly dishonest people. But, in my experience, I have seen more dishonesty from people trying to protect or isolate others from the harsh realities of the world. For example, some managers prefer to tell people what they want to hear, rather than being straightforward and honest about where they stand. This form of dishonesty is as much of a lie as dishonesty for personal gain because it prevents the truth in the form of good feedback from doing its job to help others improve.

It's true that we all lie to ourselves to some extent. We all tell ourselves things that aren't quite true. For example, while riding my bike for exercise, I sometimes tell myself I'm not very tired, and I try to convince myself that the ride is not hard. Sometimes the lie "works" (or, perhaps I was just lying to myself in assuming I was too tired) to get me through my workout. Such purposeful self-deception has a place in our lives, but the context for this skill is different.

The companion behaviors of integrity and honesty indicate that we all need to work at being honest and ethical. We all need to question our motives and examine our behaviors against reality. We all need an objective voice to help us synchronize our self-talk and improve our relations with others. This objective voice is feedback, and no one can get too much.

Shows Consideration and Concern for Others.

People who are effective at accepting feedback are also perceived as highly considerate and concerned about others. Those who rate poorly on accepting feedback also rate poorly on this companion skill. If a person shows little concern or consideration for others, then feedback from others is easily discounted. People who rate highly on concern and consideration for others are described as:

- ☐ Friendly and approachable
- ☐ Develops positive working relationships with others
- ☐ Responds to others with empathy
- ☐ When there are disagreements finds solutions that benefit both parties

In their research on change, Gene Dalton, Louis Barnes, and Abraham Zaleznik found that in order to accept feedback the feedback needs to come from a respected source.[2] No one gives much credence to feedback from people whose opinions are not valued or appreciated. A corollary to this rule is that, if a person doesn't respect those who provide feedback, that feedback will not be used to make any changes.

How often do you find that you dislike people who disagree with your opinions? Perhaps you can even see some truth in their point of view, but it is unlikely that you will acknowledge that truth unless you change your negative opinion about the person and listen to his or her feedback. For example, my son was having some difficulties with one of his teachers at school. As we discussed his class, he commented, "This teacher hates me, and I really don't like her." My son did not respect or appreciate his teacher, and his feelings made it more difficult for him to be successful in the class. It also made it easy for him to discount any feedback from the teacher.

Values Differences. People who are effective at accepting feedback also rate highly on valuing differences in others. Those who do not value differences tend to accept people and ideas that are similar to their own, while rejecting or discounting those that are different. They create for themselves a filter that discredits anything different. This automatically eliminates any feedback that does not validate their preconceived perceptions. People who rate highly on valuing differences are described as:

- ☐ Respects others; has no bias or favorites
- ☐ Open to new ideas and ways of doing things

⊡ Works effectively with people who have different points of view

When people value differences in others, they create for themselves the opportunity to value feedback from different people with different perspectives. Different perspectives or opinions threaten some people. They seek out only people who agree with their opinions.

One of the most popular TV shows is *American Idol*. The first weeks of the show include auditions by both the best and worst participants. You don't have to be an expert judge to separate those who are skilled singers from those who are not. After an individual sings, the judges give their opinion. Many of the contestants who do not sing well are shocked when they hear the judges express less-than-ecstatic remarks about their singing ability. You wonder how these people could be so self-deceived. As the dejected participants walk off the stage, they are greeted by friends and family who inevitably say things like, "What do those stupid judges know, anyway? They just can't appreciate true greatness." In reality, these friends and family have been setting up and are now reinforcing their reactions by giving the participants inaccurate (or at least heavily one-sided) feedback. Per-haps part of the problem is that the participants search out feedback only from people who will tell them what they want to hear.

Being skillful at valuing differences helps people to be more open to thoughts and ideas that are different from their own. Appreciating different ideas, perspectives, and opinions will help you gain a more accurate view of your true effectiveness.

Develops Others. People who are effective at accepting feedback also tend to be effective at developing others. When people participate in the development of others, some of that work is bound to rub off. Having the perspective that others ought to improve and develop new skills makes it much more likely that they, themselves, will be open to feedback on what they can improve. People who rate highly on developing others are described as:

- Effective at coaching others to improve
- Encourages people to continue to learn and develop themselves
- Gives honest and direct feedback
- Inspires others to achieve stretch goals
- Is committed to helping others become successful

Optimism. People who are effective at accepting feedback also tend to be optimistic. The relationship between optimism and accepting feedback is not difficult to see. Pessimists tend to view feedback as a rebuke, scolding, condemnation, or rejection because they fail to see how they can change anything. Optimists, however, tend to view feedback as a helpful suggestion or even encouragement. People who rate highly on optimism are described as:

- Has positive expectations about others
- Remains positive when given a difficult task
- Reacts positively to problems
- Maintains a positive perspective in times of crisis

Viewing feedback positively and developing the capacity to be optimistic about change or improvement will improve your ability to accept feedback.

Demonstrates Willingness to Set Stretch Goals. People who are effective at accepting feedback also tend to be more willing to set stretch goals. When people feel overwhelmed by their workload, they resist taking on additional challenges. However, although feeling overwhelmed makes people less open to feedback, such a feeling does not always correlate with actual workloads. People who rate highly on willingness to set stretch goals are described as:

- Energized to take on challenges
- Gets others to establish and pursue stretch goals
- Willingly goes above and beyond what needs to be done
- Sets high standards

Listens. People who are effective at accepting feedback also tend to have good listening skills. Poor listeners have a more difficult time accepting feedback and may not even hear or understand feedback. They begin to react to the feedback before it is fully delivered and stop listening. Good listeners take the time to really understand the feedback given, and for them, the message becomes more clarified as they listen. When people instantly react to feedback, rather than listen for clarification, they frequently walk away with the wrong message. A poor listener might hear something like, "I don't like you," when the real message being delivered is, "This work has a mistake that needs to be corrected." People who rate highly on listening skills are described as:

- Listens carefully
- Takes time to understand others' needs and problems
- Listens even if the perspectives of others are different
- Avoids criticizing others' ideas before giving them a fair hearing

Improving Companion Behaviors Helps in Accepting Feedback

By taking action to improve performance in a few of these companion behaviors, a person's ability to accept feedback is also improved. Trying to improve in all of the companion behaviors at the same time would be difficult, but improvement in any one of them will improve your ability to accept feedback. Improvement in a companion behavior also provides an additional benefit because the skills gained are core behaviors that will also improve your ability to be effective in interpersonal relationships.

Self-Assessment. Although the following exercise is not an accurate psychological assessment, it can help you identify which of the companion behaviors might be getting in the way of your ability to accept feedback. Read through each statement carefully and circle any statement you agree with, or sometimes agree with:

1 I tend to tell people what they want to hear, rather than what they need to hear.

1 Occasionally, I bend the truth in order to smooth things over with people.

1 It is almost impossible to be completely honest.

2 If the people I work with have problems or difficulties, I don't like to get involved.

2 Some people think of me as a bit standoffish.

2 If you want people to deliver on their commitments, you have to push them.

3 I like to surround myself with people who think like I do.

3 The organization is more productive when all the people think the same way.

3 It frustrates me to deal with people who have differences of opinion.

4 It bothers me when I have to spend time helping someone else develop a new skill or ability.

4 The best employees figure things out on their own, without help from others.

4 It frustrates me when I have to take time away from my work to help someone else.

5 People tend to look for problems in others.

5 When people give feedback, they are often just trying to get even.

5 People rarely change.

6 I feel overwhelmed by all the work I have to do.

6 Sometimes I feel like my job is impossible.

6 It is important to not take on more than is reasonable.

7 When listening to others, I rarely ask additional questions to clarify what people have said.

7 I usually find myself thinking about how I am going to respond when I am listening to another person.

7 I occasionally get accused of not listening well to others.

Count up the number of times you circled an item. The questions are linked to the following companion behaviors:

1 Integrity and honesty

2 Shows consideration and concern for others

3 Values differences

4 Develops others

5 Optimism

6 Demonstrates willingness to set stretch goals

7 Listens

If you circled two or three items in any one of the seven companion behaviors, this behavior is a significant impediment in your ability to accept feedback. If you find that a companion behavior gets in the way of your accepting feedback, consider some of your past experiences and circumstances where problems occurred. You could also ask others to help you understand how that behavior impacts them. To accomplish this, ask a person who is not afraid to be candid and honest with you, and ask that person for his or her honest perceptions of the problem (or the person may only tell you what you want to hear). Once you understand the problem and when it occurs, you can begin to create a plan for change. Refer to Chapters 7 and 8 in this book for additional insights.

As you make changes, you will not only notice that your willingness to accept feedback improves, but you are receiving more feedback (both positive and negative) from others. Once people recognize that you are open and willing to accept feedback, then more feedback becomes available. You will find that feedback becomes a great asset in your life. You will have greater clarity about your strengths and weakness, and you will understand when your attempts to influence and communicate with others really work, or fail miserably. Without feedback, you will never know and therefore cannot improve. Accepting and responding to feedback is the most significant variable affecting a person's ability to be effective on an interpersonal level.

4

Why Change?

As soon as people receive feedback, they frequently begin to wrestle with the question, "Why should I change?" Do you identify with any of the following negative attitudes that are common after receiving feedback?

- "I paid my dues when I was younger. Now that I've achieved my position, I deserve a break."
- "I shouldn't be expected to respond to every little request."
- "If others can't accept me with a few weaknesses, that's their problem. I've done my best, and I deserve a little latitude."
- "When I was young, I learned the ropes. Now I teach others the ropes."
- "I know I'm not perfect, but my strengths clearly outweigh my weaknesses."

When we think about personal development and change, we tend to think that childhood or adolescence was the time for most significant changes to occur. We usually believe that, as adults, we are more stable and mature—that perhaps we might have to pass through some minor refinements, but not the kinds of major changes we went through in our youth.

Feedback usually gives us some good news and some bad news. Most people are willing to acknowledge their weaknesses, but they do not always try to improve them. The comment heard most often by facilitators when reviewing feedback with participants is, "I knew I had a problem in this area." Occasionally feedback comes as a big surprise, but most of the time, people have known about their weaknesses for some time, often for years. I ask, "If you already knew about this problem, why didn't you do something about it?" They inevitably answer, "It didn't seem that important," or, "I didn't want to." The problem is not that people can't change. The problem is that they do not want to change badly enough. Figure 4.1

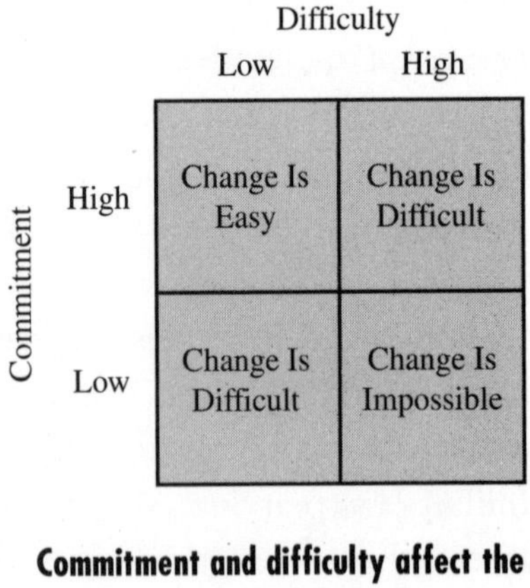

Figure 4.1   Commitment and difficulty affect the possibility of change.

illustrates the dynamics of change around commitment and difficulty.

PRINCIPLE 15

Change is only easy when you combine a high level of commitment with a low degree of difficulty.

When commitment is high and the difficulty of a task is high, making a change is going to be difficult. But, even when the difficulty of a task is low, if commitment is low, making a change is still difficult. However, when commitment is low and the difficulty of a task is high, making a change is virtually impossible.

Performance Expectations

Before you begin to try to make some changes, you should first understand a few things about yourself. First, change does not happen automatically. Simply acknowledging the existence of a problem (though an excellent place to start), does not change the problem. The first key to making lasting changes is to increase your level of motivation and commitment to making the change. Without commitment, only the easiest issues can be resolved, and then only with some difficulty.

In biology, the law of homeostasis describes how equilibrium is maintained in a body. Bodies maintain balance in their systems through self-regulated, internal mechanisms.[1] A similar thing happens in the workplace. As people master their jobs, they typically try to achieve a comfortable and consistent level of performance, or performance homeostasis. And because they now have increased knowledge and skills, doing an effective job requires less effort and stress than when the job began.

PRINCIPLE 16

Over time, people tend to maintain the same level of performance that they had when they first mastered their job.

Most people strive for performance homeostasis. As they consider their performance, they often justify such a state by pointing out how they continue to perform at the same levels, if not at higher levels than they did in previous years. The *law of performance homeostasis* predicts that most people would rather perform their jobs in a relaxed and comfortable state than in a stressed-out, exhausted state.

Most of us believe we have to "pay our dues." But once we have paid them, do we have to continue to pay them? As we look back on our lives, we usually look to school as the time when we paid our dues. And, perhaps the first few years of work served as additional payment. We look forward to the time when we can generate excellent performance without much effort, and reap the reward with a higher paycheck. Things would work out fine except for one major problem—expectations! The longer you work, the higher the expectations others have about what you can do. The more you know, the more others expect you to know. The more you do in a day, the more others expect you to do in a day.

PRINCIPLE 17

To maintain a perception of high performance, you must change over time.

Since expectations increase over time, performing at the same levels and doing the same kind of work throughout your career predictably results in lower performance evaluations from others as time goes on.

Many people fantasize that, because of their hard work in the past, they can produce excellent work in the future with very little effort. (This fantasy resides in the same area of the brain as the one about the investment we can make for pennies that soon will be worth millions, and we only have to make the decision to buy at the right time.) The problem with such a performance fantasy is the increasing expectation. Others will always want and expect more.

We must change our basic philosophy about work and leave behind the desire to "take it easy." A new philosophy must embrace continuous change, growth, and development. In the same way that exercise makes us strong and preserves and enhances our lifestyle, the changes we make on the job can have dramatic positive effects.

We should replace our goals of performance homeostasis with goals of increasing contribution. Rather than looking forward to the point where we can sit back and relax, we should set goals to contribute even more in the future. Since performance expectations increase over time, if we allow gaps to form between what others expect of us and what we contribute, then we become easy targets for downsizing and layoffs.

Many people believe that the simplest way to increase your contribution is to work harder, since hard work will be valued and noticed by others. But increasing your workload beyond your capacity only leads to anxiety and burnout. Over the long term, the only sane way to increase your contribution is to change the way you work: Work smarter, not harder.

Average Isn't Good Enough

Clients frequently ask my company to review survey results to identify the one or two main issues that separate highly satisfied and motivated teams from dissatisfied and unmotivated teams. Most often, the leading factor in group motivation and satisfaction is the effectiveness of a group's supervisor. After performing such a study in one organization, the company's management went on a "witch hunt" to find and eliminate the ineffective, "terrible" group of supervisors. But, although the company identified a few supervisors who could be classified as "bad," most of the company's supervisors were "average."

One manager said, "I was expecting to interview highly controlling, insensitive bullies, but I found that most of the supervisors who were ineffective were nice. Some of them were my buddies. I just didn't think they were that bad; and in fact, they weren't bad. They were just average."

At first, management questioned the study's validity, but, after further examination, the frightening truth became clear:

PRINCIPLE 18

"Average" managers are not good enough to make a significant impact on employee satisfaction and motivation.

People who would never be satisfied with average ratings on objective measures (such as grades in school, test scores, or profitability) often consider average to be acceptable on subjective, perceptual measures such as feedback from others, since those measures seem to be more open to personal interpretation. But remember: *Perceptions are reality.* Some people rationalize that average performance in some areas is due to excellent performance in others. But it was shown previously that excellent performance in critical areas has a halo effect on performance. Thus, because of high performance in those critical areas, overall ratings for these people tend to be much higher than average.

However, the problem is that critical performance factors change over time. An area that may not have been critical in the past becomes critical in the future. In the same way that a positive halo effect follows excellent performance in critical areas, a negative halo effect surrounds poor performance in those same areas. Poor performance in critical areas weighs like an iron anchor on the perceptions of others.

Average is never good enough to create excellence, and seeking to maintain average performance promotes mediocrity. As long as everyone else is average and the demand for workers exceeds the supply, then average performance may provide some job security. But, as employees begin to differentiate themselves by excellent performance in critical areas, especially in a down economy, average performance begins to look bad.

PRINCIPLE 19

Everything you do makes a difference.

I find it amusing to go out to dinner with people who are on diets. Some rigidly stick to their diets, but most people, when tempted with high-fat entrées or desserts, typically make one of the following excuses:

- ☐ It doesn't count if you eat it before 6 P.M.
- ☐ It doesn't count if you eat it with your meal.
- ☐ It doesn't count if you exercise after you eat it.

As we all know, one of the harsh realities of life (that most of us don't want to accept) is that everything counts. If mistakes or embarrassing experiences occur, they may be small, they may be forgotten, but they do count. Luckily this phenomenon works both ways: Small, positive events also count.

As you consider the feedback you receive, you might say to yourself that a particular issue is not significant, or that it doesn't count. But it does count. It may not count much, looking at the weakness in light of all your strengths, and it may seem totally insignificant, but it definitely counts. Highly effective people believe this; average people do not.

Begin Where You Are

As Tom considered his survey results, it became evident to him that others perceived he lacked the ability to think and act strategically. He reacted by explaining that his job didn't require or encourage him to think strategically: "I just carry out the orders my boss gives me and run my function the way it has always been run," and continued by saying that, if he'd had a job that required him to think strategically, he could be as strategic as the president of the company. He thought the data was more a reflection of his position than his ability.

The facilitator asked Tom which jobs in the company required strategic thinking. He named a few. The facilitator then asked him if managers in the company would ever consider a person for one of those positions who they felt did not have the ability to think and act strategically. He said no.

The facilitator said, "Tom, you're never going to get the job that requires you to act strategically until you can demonstrate to others that you can think strategically."

So often, people say, "I will change when my situation changes." One nonmanager asked, "How can I show people how well I can lead, when I don't have anyone to lead?" The problem is management always looks for the person it knows will be a good leader. The burden of proof is on the prospective leader, not on management. Workers must find a way to demonstrate their leadership abilities in nonmanagement positions.

Change has to start now, in the present job and in the current situation. In the previous example, for Tom to be considered for a job at the next level, he needs to begin now to think and act strategically. For workers to be considered for management positions, they must demonstrate that they can lead in the positions where they are now.

You Are Part of a Larger System

In our culture, we have a tremendous tendency to assign blame. It starts at a very early age. For example, if I ask my children who made a mess in the living room, they point the finger at another brother or sister. Similarly, I am always amazed that, when managers encounter complex and difficult problems, they frequently solve them by replacing somebody. The problem is still there, but now they have someone to blame. I am not only amazed by our tendency to blame others, but also by our willingness to accept all the blame ourselves. "I blew it; I'm responsible," a manager once told me as we discussed a problem. It's as if life would be simpler for everyone if someone else could just take all the responsibility.

Performance problems are a function of three things:

1. The person (including the person's ability, character, attitude, etc.)
2. The environment or situation of the work group (the kind of work, the setting, interaction with other groups, organizational factors, etc.)
3. The people who interact with the person (bosses, peers, those who report to the person, etc.)

PRINCIPLE 20

Involving others in your efforts to change increases the likelihood that change will occur.

Codependence, an idea currently used in helping alcoholics overcome their addictions, may offer some insight into resolving performance problems. The basic notion of codependence is that alcoholics have drinking problems not only because of an inability to cope with alcohol, but also because their relationships with others tend to reinforce their method of facing problems.

In treating alcoholism in the past, before codependence was identified, patients would be taken out of their homes, placed in institutions for several months, and then moved into outpatient programs for several more months. The assumption was that alcoholics had a problem they needed to change, and that those who were not alcoholics did not have a problem and did not need to change. But when the alcoholics were released from the institutions, they returned to the same environments they had left, including the same people, the same situations, and the same method of facing problems. And the alcoholics' ability to cope had not changed. This approach did not take into consideration the people who were not alcoholics, who may have contributed to the problems that provoked the alcoholics to turn to alcohol in the first place.

New approaches that consider codependence recognize that alcoholics are just one part of a complex social system. Alcoholism occurs in part because of an inability to control drinking, but also in part because those who live and work with the alcoholic often help to generate the circumstances that make alcoholics want to escape to alcohol. Although it is helpful to teach alcoholics how to cope with problems on their own, it is usually more helpful to get a group of people working together to solve problems. By understanding that much of the problem has to do with interpersonal relationships, therapists work not only with the alcoholics, but also with spouses and family members, and with those who live and work with them.

The problem for the alcoholics is that they drink; the problem with the others is that their interactions tend to cause the alcoholics to want to drink. The therapist helps family members understand how their behaviors may influence the alcoholic to continue drinking. When everyone in the family changes, it is far more likely that the alcoholic will also change.

So where does the idea of codependence fit in the workplace? For the average person, asking others for help is often perceived as a sign of weakness. Most of us view ourselves as rugged individualists making our own decisions, charting our own courses, and mapping out our own futures. We tend to underestimate the influence of others on our decisions and actions. One of the best ways to learn new skills and better ways to interact with others is from a coach or mentor—someone we can observe, who has the right skills and who will observe us and provide feedback, encouragement, and suggestions for change.

Attitudes about Change

In a survey of 500 employees in a major corporation, we asked if employees felt that in the past year their company had undergone too much change. The majority indicated that the company had experienced too much change. The company was facing some difficult realities: declining market share, increasing utilization of new technology among competitors, and falling stock prices. Therefore, reducing the amount of change in the company would have been equivalent to going out of business in the near future. The company had to make some enormous changes just to stay competitive.

The pace and scale of change continue to grow in all aspects of modern life. The art of changing individual or collective behaviors has become a very useful survival skill in these times. Learning to change begins with the right attitude toward change. Some of the following attitudes may help you as you navigate the change process:

1. *If I am not changing and improving, I am standing still (or possibly even degenerating).* With the right attitude, change is exhilarating and exciting. It makes life

interesting. A difficult circumstance can be described either as a disaster or as an adventure. When I interview executives who demonstrate exceptional skills and abilities, I ask them how they develop their great talents. The story I hear over and over again is, "I was given a new job or assignment that was a huge challenge. I did not have the skills to succeed, but it was sink or swim. I tried hard. I got lots of feedback. But, over time, I developed the talent." So, depending on your attitude, difficult circumstances can provide the opportunity for a person to learn new skills, or they can provide a miserable experience in futility.

2 *Change is a skill I can master.* You probably remember learning to ride a bike. You probably did not succeed on your first try. But, after some difficulty, you suddenly "got it." Mastering change is very similar, but it generally takes a lot longer to master. Talk to people who are masters of change, and what you will find is that they practiced, and practiced, and practiced.

3 *There will never come a time in which some change will not be useful.* One of the most difficult changes people make is retirement and old age. Becoming a master of change before you reach these periods in your life will be a great benefit to you.

4 *Successful people continually change and improve.* Failures do not need to change at all. Research has shown that the longer people are in a job, the higher the expectations become for their performance. Organizations expect a greater contribution out of someone who has been in a job for five years than they do for someone

who has only been there for one year. Problems occur when expectations exceed actual performance. The reality of having a productive career is that you must continually look for new ways to add value and increase your effectiveness. It is not enough to work harder or longer, because those ideas are both limiting. The key to career success is finding new and different ways to contribute, and this requires change.

5

Deciding What to Change

Several years ago, I arrived home late from an out-of-town trip. As I slipped quietly into bed, I noticed a note on my pillow. I slipped into the bathroom, thinking it must be a love note from my wife. As I turned on the bathroom light, I read in large print on the cover page of the note: "Things You Can Do to Save Our Marriage."

This got my attention.

When I turned to the next page, I saw a list of 24 items. At the top of the list, in the number one position, was "Clean Your Office."

The next day, I got up early and spent most of the day cleaning and organizing my office. By the time I finished, it was perfect. My wife was impressed by my efforts, and so I thought I would not have to worry too much about the other 23 items.

I kept my office clean for a few weeks, and then asked my wife for some feedback. Her response was clear and to the point: "Nothing has changed," she said.

"But, what about the office?" I asked. With that, she just looked at me in disgust and walked away.

What I have found since then is that, even though the cluttered appearance of my office may be a frequent grumble for my wife, its cleanliness has almost no correlation to the quality of our marriage. My office can be a disaster at the same time our marriage seems wonderful, or it can be very clean and organized even when our marriage is experiencing frustrations.

I found that the issue at the top of the list was not necessarily the most important one to change. I also found that other items on the list had a much more direct and significant correlation to the quality of our marriage. Some of these items included helping out more with children and not being critical of my wife's decisions and actions. I learned from this experience that I had been paying the most attention to the things that others complained about the most or the loudest or that were at the top of the list. What got my attention and was complained about most frequently was not necessarily the most important issue to change.

PRINCIPLE 21

The most critical skill in making change based on feedback is deciding what specific issue to work on first.

Many feedback experiences are very similar. Often, people identify the issue that appears to be the most negative and conclude it is the most important issue to change. This is faulty logic. Issues that are most negative or most complained about are simply the ones that are most noticeable. Evaluating what issues to change ought to be a completely separate decision-making process, independent from how negatively people react to issues.

In a perfect world, we would receive feedback on many issues and change everything appropriately. We would soon become perfect ourselves. But in the real world, people face limitations in terms of how many issues they can successfully address at a time. A guaranteed way to fail in making changes based on feedback is trying to change too many things at the same time.

People cannot make five major changes at the same time. In fact, whenever most people try to change more than one or two important things at once, they end up making no changes at all. In a recent project, we asked the leaders in an organization to focus their efforts for change on only one issue. As we measured the level of improvement after six months, we found a significant difference between the pre- and posttest measures. Most people worry that if they focus only on changing one issue, others will not notice. But others do notice a difference. In fact, the larger the difference, the more they notice. Spreading your efforts between several change efforts may prevent people from noticing that things are changing, because they will see little difference between where you started and where you are now. Focusing your efforts on changing one issue increases the likelihood that people will see a difference.

Managing Expectations

Change is difficult. It requires focused effort and attention. Most change efforts do not occur in a vacuum. We still have to complete our required work and take care of ourselves and our families. However, focused effort on a few specific issues greatly improves the likelihood of success. It is critical that you learn how to prioritize issues discovered through feedback according to which will yield the greatest benefit.

The people whom you ask for feedback will likely expect you to take action on all of their feedback. It is helpful to establish up front that, although they may provide feedback on a variety of issues, you will focus your efforts on selected issues as you work your way through the feedback. To manage these expectations, follow these four steps:

1. Thank anyone and everyone who gave you feedback.
2. Even though you may not be able to respond to every issue, acknowledge that you have received the feedback and that it is valid.
3. Tell the people who gave you feedback that you intend to focus on one or two of the most critical issues.
4. Find a way to demonstrate that you are changing.

Although people would like you to change everything based on their feedback, their experience leads them to believe little change will actually take place. When you make a focused effort to change a few critical issues, people will be better able to see change and won't focus on the issues not yet addressed.

Prioritizing Issues

To prioritize issues, rate each issue against three criteria: felt need, ease of change, and relative impact.

Felt Need. The first step in bringing about change is to create a felt need for change. As you think about the issues for which you received negative feedback, you may notice one issue for which others feel a high need for you to change, but you feel little or no need to change. How can you increase your felt need?

As you think about issues raised through feedback, ask yourself the extent to which you have a high, medium, or low felt need to change this issue. Do not confuse your felt need for change with the needs and desires of others. If others feel we need to change and we do not, then we can only talk about changing, or make a show of changing—but we won't change. In their extensive research on change, Gene Dalton, Louis Barnes, and Abraham Zaleznik report that having a high felt need for change is the most important factor in predicting whether change will occur. They describe the classic example of the felt need of an alcoholic in the following scenario:[1]

The wife of a man with a drinking problem asked him to go to Alcoholics Anonymous (AA). The man went to an AA meeting.

The leader of the group asked the man if he was an alcoholic. The man said, "No, I don't think I am. But my wife thinks I have a problem."

The group leader replied, "Why don't you go drink some more because we can't do anything to help you until you think you have a problem."

For each of the issues for which you receive negative feedback, ask yourself which issues you would most like to change. Make sure you separate your desires from the desires of others. If your boss has placed a great deal of pressure on you to change a particular behavior, determine whether your need to change is driven by you or by your boss.

The "not invented here" syndrome is the most fundamental hurdle that keeps people from developing a strong felt need for change. You have the "not invented here" syndrome when you say things like, "My boss thinks I need to change this," or, "Other people think I have a problem in this area." In these situations, your real felt need is not to change the problem, but to change other people's opinions about the problem. One way to avoid the "not invented here" syndrome is to *reinvent* negative feedback. Take the feedback you received and restate it in your own words, thoughts, and feelings.

Start the reinvention process by examining how you look at a particular issue, being totally honest with yourself in terms of the impact this issue has on you and others. Try to understand why others become frustrated by the issue while you don't. Is this an issue that negatively impacts other people more than it does you?

If you cannot reinvent the feedback and take ownership of the perceptions and feelings of others, you will feel no need to change that issue. Your felt need for change may be lower than others' for two reasons: First, you don't understand the impact the issue has on others; or, second, you understand the impact, but you simply don't care as much as others do. It frequently helps to have frank, open discussions with others about the issues, especially the ones for which you continue to feel little or no need to change.

After reviewing the feedback received from her peers, Angela decided her problem was not her behavior, but rather her peers' lack of understanding of the situation. She arranged to have lunch with each of them to talk about their feedback and help them understand her situation.

At lunch, Angela thanked each of her peers for their feedback and then described her own view of the situation. Each of her peers listened patiently, and then, one by one, they informed Angela that they had been aware of her situation. But this fact did not change the relevance of their feedback. They reinforced to Angela that she needed to change her own behavior, even though the situation made it difficult.

By the time Angela had taken four of her peers to lunch, her felt need to change had become high enough for her to pursue the issue and change her behavior.

Your need for change is affected by two perspectives: First, how the issue negatively affects you and your associates (the *push*), and, second, how making the change will have a positive impact (the *pull*). Most often, we focus our attention on the push, or the negative impact.

But the pull can provide greater motivation. If you understand only the negative impact of your behavior and have no sense of the positive impact of change, you will find less motivation to change and therefore have a lower felt need. As you focus on the pull, you begin to consider the benefits of making a change. This change of focus can turn guilt into proactivity and frustration into action.

Ease of Change.   Some issues are easier to change than others. In planning your change process, select at least one issue you know will be easy to change. This not only gives you confidence in your ability to change, but it sends a positive signal to others that you have responded to their feedback. For example, job skills and time management are generally easier to change than personality traits. (Figure 5.1 provides some helpful guidelines to use in judging the ease of change.)

Issues	Ease of Change
Job skills	
Organization and time management	
Management of work	Easier
Technical knowledge	
Behaviors	
Attitudes and stereotypes	
Habits	
Personality traits	Harder
Culture and values	

Figure 5.1   Relative ease of change.

THE POWER OF FEEDBACK

After we form an overall impression of a person, we adjust our feedback on various characteristics to fit our overall impression. We also use a "packaging" approach (a general impression to attribute a broader set of characteristics) to provide feedback to others. Frequently, however, we make attributions based on a few specific behaviors and determine that a person has a certain personality characteristic.

Suppose you observe someone who frequently arrives late to meetings, and you strongly believe that being late for meetings is irresponsible. You also observe that when your boss tries to assign a job to that person, that person pushes back, asking the boss to assign the job to someone else. You conclude, based on the observed behaviors, that the person is irresponsible. When you have a chance to provide feedback to this person, you write several comments such as: "Unwilling to take on necessary responsibilities," and "Irresponsible and lacks true commitment to the company."

"Irresponsibility" is a personality trait that is very difficult to change whereas "arriving late for meetings" is a time management behavior that is relatively easy to change.

Most of us are not always clear about how we form our conclusions. Most of the time we provide feedback based on our overall impression and the packaged bundle of traits that fit the impression, instead of on the specific behaviors that led us to our conclusions. Clarity regarding what needs to be changed can significantly improve a person's chance of changing.

PRINCIPLE 22

Issues dealing with things are easier to change than issues dealing with people.

Another thing to consider in rating the difficulty of change is whether the matter deals with people or things. For example, correcting a "bug" in a software program is easier to change than managing a conflict between you and another person. Changing things is easier than changing people for two reasons: First, we have much more control over things. Things do not resist or reject changes, as people often do. And, second, we are more skillful at working with things than with people.

Kerri received some very specific negative feedback about her ability to manage conflicts between two of the people who reported to her and who worked closely together. This upset her because she had spent much of her time and energy working on the issues with both of them.

Finally, in frustration, Kerri changed the job assignment and workstation of one of the people, moving the person to another part of the building. After a week of grumbling about the new arrangements, the two stopped their contentions, and their conflict never came up again.

Changes that involve others do not need to be difficult, if we apply different skills in the way we deal with people.

Relative Impact

We tend to think that effective people have excellent skills in every area—that they are "excellent at everything." But after studying many profiles of highly rated leaders, we found that the "excellent at everything" notion does not hold true.

Feedback profiles show that highly rated leaders are excellent at a few things and good or average at most other things. Also, when we look at the feedback profiles of the lowest rated leaders, we do not find them to be terrible at everything. Their profiles show poor performance in one or two critical areas, but the poor performance in critical areas has a negative halo effect on other skills.

The most critical question in prioritizing issues is: "If you were to change one issue, which one would make the most significant difference in how you are perceived?" When you make changes on high-impact issues, others notice a big change. But when you change a low-impact issue, others either do not notice the change or they do not see it as very important. To evaluate the relative impact of a change, you need to ask and answer two questions:

1. Which issues are most important?
2. How effective do I need to be at an individual issue?

Which Issues Are Most Important? To assess the relative impact of a change, you first need to distinguish between essential, necessary, and nonessential skills, knowledge, and activities:

- *Essential skills, knowledge, and activities,* if demonstrated well, lead others to perceive high performance.
- *Necessary skills, knowledge, and activities* are those that need to be performed and are a required part of

the job, but they are not as closely linked to perceived high performance. These traits help attain high performance and require good or average execution, and cannot be ignored. But demonstrating excellence in these areas will not convince others you are exceptional.

On an interpersonal level, personal hygiene is a good example. We all need to maintain personal hygiene that others deem appropriate. For example, a male without a beard needs to shave daily. Some men who have dark or heavy beards may need to shave again in the evening to avoid a five-o'clock shadow. Coming to work unshaven may be perceived as inappropriate in many office situations. But, if you were to shave several times a day, would it make a difference to anyone? No! No one would notice, nor would they care. In fact, taking time to shave might pull you away from other tasks. Shaving is necessary, but not essential for leveraging high performance.

- *Nonessential skills, knowledge, and activities* are things that are not required, nor are they linked to high performance as perceived by others. These things may be important to you or to the execution of other jobs, but they do not impact your perceived performance on the observed job. Most people feel they perform very few nonessential activities, but in reality, many of us do. We may feel a particular activity is important, but others fail to see its value.

How Effective Do You Need to Be?

Make a list of your 20 most important skills, areas of knowledge, and activities. Then classify each item as "essential," "necessary," or "nonessential."

Most people classify 18 of their 20 activities as "essential," but, since they do not completely understand how "essential" differs from "necessary," they disperse their effectiveness and try to exert equal effort on essential and necessary areas. Bosses and peers tend to understand the differences even less. If you ask them what is essential, they tend to respond that everything is essential. We gain greater clarity through study and negotiation with others, rather than by simply asking. The process begins when you have determined what is essential.

From your list of activities, knowledge areas, and skills, choose five that you feel are most essential. To help you make the selection, ask yourself the following questions:

1. Which of these skills or activities could I perform at an average or good level and still be considered a top performer overall?
2. If I only did one or two of these things well, which one would make the biggest difference or have the most significant impact on the way others perceive my performance?
3. Which activities, skills, or areas of knowledge do people notice and recognize when I do them well?

4. Which one or two activities would my boss, peers, or direct reports place in the nonessential category?
5. Which skill, area of knowledge, or activity is most highly correlated with my ability to influence my central mission?

Most jobs have a central mission or activity along with many secondary activities. Think about your central mission and activities, and then differentiate those from secondary activities. Learn which activities, skills, and areas of knowledge other people perceive to make the highest impact. You may discover a significant difference between what you think is important and what others perceive as important. Focusing your efforts on areas you feel are important, but that others do not value, only compounds the problem of perceived poor performance. If you think some issues are essential, but others do not, your performance won't be perceived positively. You then focus your time and energy on activities that others don't feel are important. Paying attention to activities that make a difference is critical.

Reach an agreement with your boss, peers, and direct reports about which activities are essential. Frequently, this consensus comes through negotiation. Other times it comes when you accept the views of others about what is important. The end result of the exercise is that you clarify which activities are essential, necessary, and nonessential.

Finally, link your feedback to the list. Sometimes there is a one-to-one correlation. For example, you may find that technical product knowledge is identified as essential, and you in fact received feedback about needing to improve your technical product knowledge or indicating a new area of strength. Other times, the correlation may be ambiguous: You may receive negative feedback on listening skills, but you find it is linked to several activities on your list. Whenever feedback issues are not directly linked to one skill, knowledge, or activity, identify the one or two issues having the most significant correlation. Be sure to link both areas of improvement and perceived strengths to the activities. (Table 5.1 helps establish the correlation between essential, necessary, and nonessential areas and the feedback you receive.)

After completing the table, you will find it easy to assign different levels of importance to each of the feedback items. You may need more time to complete the table if you still need to negotiate the importance levels with others.

Bill finished his rating activity and found that his view of what was important differed significantly from the views of others. He explained, "Others simply can't appreciate my job for what it is," and he knew he was right. He felt it would be critical to develop breadth in a variety of technical areas, and that such breadth would provide him with added insight into how his work integrated with the work of other professionals. Although his peers and his boss saw value in increasing the breadth of his activities, they also noted a significant problem in how he went about developing breadth.

Table 5.1   Essential Activities Worksheet

List of Skills, Knowledge, Activities	Essential	Necessary	Nonessential	Correlation with Feedback Issues

Bill had unique skills in one technology. One-third of the company's profits depended on having skills in that technology. But in the past year, Bill had focused 75 percent of his efforts on gaining expertise in other areas. People inside and outside the company began to notice Bill's lack of attention to his own area. His peers, some of whom were experts in the other areas, did not completely understand his motives. Some of them thought he might be trying to take over their jobs.

His rating activity led to a discussion between Bill and his boss. After the meeting, Bill resolved to change his emphasis to a 25 percent effort in other areas, and he committed to help his peers develop skills in that area, as well.

The feedback Bill had received became clearer as the rating process unfolded. Negative comments such as "lack of patience," "pushy," and "not customer-oriented" made more sense to him, given his new orientation toward what was important in his job.

How Good Is Good Enough?

A cost-benefit analysis of a manufacturing process showed that, as the costs of increasing the purity of a material increased, the benefits derived from the increased strength and appearance of the final product decreased. Individual skills can be viewed in the same light. Sometimes good performance in one skill is all that is necessary. Absolute excellence would not produce any noticeable effects or impact.

A person's performance and effectiveness are usually judged in comparison to others. Your performance relative to others may be described in three ways:

1. *Competitive advantage:* Excellent performance compared to others, well above average.
2. *Parity:* Performance at about the same level as others, average.
3. *Competitive disadvantage:* Inadequate performance compared to others, well below average.

If a particular issue is essential and your performance gives you a competitive advantage, you should work to maintain that level of effectiveness. If your performance is average, you should work to improve your effectiveness. If you feel you have a competitive disadvantage, you should begin to make major changes. Before you begin to evaluate your performance by these three definitions, first determine the level of perceived importance others have assigned. For levels of performance that you would describe as on parity with others, and which you find are necessary (but not essential) in importance, you should maintain your current level of effectiveness. For performance that gives you a competitive disadvantage, with a necessary importance level, you need to improve. However, having a competitive disadvantage on nonessential issues makes no difference to your perceived performance, and you should not invest much energy in improving performance in these areas. (Figure 5.2 shows how to combine importance ratings with individual effectiveness.)

		Importance	
Effectiveness	Essential	Necessary	Nonessential
Competitive Advantage	Maintain	OK	OK
Average Performance	Improve	Maintain	OK
Competitive Disadvantage	Major Change	Improve	Maintain

Figure 5.2 Effectiveness and importance ratings indicate how you can prioritize your efforts.

Prioritization Worksheet

Use Table 5.2 to list the most negative issues from your feedback. Rate the criteria "high," "medium," or "low," according to your felt need, ease of change, and relative impact.

Table 5.2   Prioritization Worksheet

List of Issues	Felt Need	Ease of Change	Relative Impact

After you complete the prioritization worksheet, you should have a better idea of what you should work on. As you select issues to work on, consider these four criteria:

1. *Do not select more than two issues to work on at a time.* In fact, for best results, select only one. You will find tremendous power in focusing all of your energy for change on fewer issues. Although you may feel tempted to select more than two issues, do not fall into the trap of taking on too much.

2. *If the two issues you select are both difficult to change, consider selecting one issue that will be easier.* Look for a quick win with one issue. This not only sends a positive message to others, but it also provides you with some needed confidence.

3. *Do not select an issue that others want changed more than you do.* Until your felt need matches others' felt need, your odds of making a lasting change are significantly reduced.

4. *Find one essential issue that will give you a competitive advantage.*

6

Fixing Weaknesses or Building Strengths?

In a study of the factors that underlie leadership failures, Jack Zenger and I reviewed the feedback assessments of leaders described as "failing."[1] After reviewing the data, it became clear that those leaders were doing something wrong. It was also clear that feedback surveys could accurately identify significant problems to those who were failing, and that those people should pay close attention to the feedback and work hard to make corrections. The data showed, for example, if an individual had received significant negative evaluations on critical competencies, that person's overall perceived effectiveness was very low. On the surface, the study seemed to reinforce our approach of encouraging people to identify and accept feedback on weaknesses and then work on improving those weaknesses.

But something else came up: We analyzed the feedback assessments of hundreds of leaders who had been evaluated on 17 core competencies. It turned out that only 21 percent of the leaders had one or more of the competencies rated as a weakness. As we reviewed other data sets from 360-degree feedback surveys, it appeared that the percentage of leaders with a weakness in one of the core competencies ranges from about 12 percent to 25 percent. After reviewing thousands of 360-degree feedback reports, we found that, although some people receive strong negative data, the majority of feedback assessments with negative items might be more accurately characterized as "less positive."

Even though leaders frequently receive feedback that is not extremely negative, they continue to focus their efforts for change on the "least positive" items.

"Isn't That What We're Supposed to Do?"

I recently met with a group of 25 director level managers to conduct a training program. I asked them, "How many of you have had 360-degree feedback in the past?" Every hand went up. I then asked, "How many of you focused your efforts for change on the most negative areas identified in the survey?" Again, every hand went up. I asked them why they did that. The consensus of the group was:

- "Isn't that what we're supposed to do?"
- "Isn't that what people want us to do?"
- "Isn't that how you improve?"

People universally concede that the best way to improve personal performance is to work on eliminating weaknesses. I have not found any group or culture or country where this idea isn't a standard belief. This belief is reinforced by experiences in our families, education, training, and performance reviews. It seems silly to even question the assumption that the best way to improve is to work on our weaknesses.

PRINCIPLE 23

Most people believe that, to improve, they have to eliminate their weaknesses rather than build on their strengths.

To show some contrast to this thinking, I ask the groups I work with to participate in a little experiment. I ask them as a group to think of a great leader, and then I ask the group what makes that leader great. Most groups have no difficulty coming up with a list of profound strengths. I then ask them if this leader had any weaknesses, since every great leader seems to have a few. Again, most groups find it fairly easy to generate a short list of weaknesses. Finally, I ask them to tell me why those weaknesses don't seem to matter very much. The universal answer is, "Because their strengths are so profound." After conducting this experiment hundreds of times, I realized that advising people to work on improving their weaknesses is only good advice if one of the weaknesses is a "fatal flaw." The key to improving individual effectiveness is developing a few profound strengths.

The Fear of Embarrassment

As I have tried to understand the need most people seem to have to work on their weaknesses, I reflected on a recurring dream I'd had back in grade school. In the dream, I was standing on a ledge in the school cafeteria in my underwear. The other children were looking at me and pointing, and I was completely humiliated. (When I got to college, I was surprised and somewhat relieved to find in a psychology text that this dream is actually quite common among adolescents.) This dream identifies one of our basic human fears—the fear of being considered incompetent. I believe one of the reasons we work so hard on fixing our less positive issues is we don't want to be embarrassed by our weaknesses.

For most people, the logic is to identify their most glaring weakness (or "least positive" trait) and continually work to improve on that issue. Then they look for the next weakness and work on that one. They reason that through this process they will continually improve themselves over time. But this approach poses a few problems. First, people are continually working to improve themselves on issues they usually don't care much about.

Think about something big you have been able to change in your life (e.g., quitting smoking, having success on a diet, starting and maintaining a new exercise routine, getting out of a bad relationship). Were you able to make this change in your life without passion, energy, or commitment? For most people, the answer would be a resounding no. Big changes are not easy; they require enormous effort. By working on changing issues that are least positive, people typically face issues for which they have little passion.

In reviewing the 360-degree feedback results with Melissa, the facilitator pointed to the most negative item and asked her, "Melissa, don't you think you should address that issue."
Melissa replied, "Oh yeah, that! I always get that feedback. Sure, I guess I ought to do something to improve, because that issue is a constant thorn in my side."

With a response like that, what do you think will happen when Melissa takes action? She will try; she will put forth some effort, but it doesn't sound like she has much passion, or excitement, or motivation. In working on their least positive issues, most people end up investing their time and effort in changing issues for which they have little passion—with the net result being little change.

Focusing on Strengths

After I spoke on this topic to a group of navy officers in Washington, DC, a captain came up to me and told me about his son who had a learning disability. The disability caused his son to struggle in his English classes with reading and spelling. At 16, he finished his junior year in high school, and his parents considered putting him in summer school to get him some additional help in reading and spelling so he could prepare for his college entrance exams. Before signing up, however, they had him evaluated by a psychologist. The parents asked the psychologist if it would be wise to put their son in summer school, where he could focus on reading and spelling.

The psychologist told them, "If you put him in summer school to work on English, two things will happen: One, he won't learn much; and two, he will probably hate you for it."

The parents replied, "Well, he might hate us now, but he will thank us later." But they asked the psychologist why he thought their son would not learn much.

The psychologist said that he felt their son was about as good in reading and spelling as he was going to get. Then he said, "I do have another suggestion: Your son is very gifted in math, and he enjoys math. My guess is that, if you put him in summer school to study math, he will hit the 80th or 90th percentile on his college entrance tests—and, not only that, he will probably enjoy summer school instead of hating the experience."

The parents chose to put their son in summer school to study math, and after high school he was accepted into an excellent college.

What "No Strength" Means to Effectiveness

The alternative to working on weaknesses is to build on strengths. This approach might seem misguided— what's the point of improving something you are already good at doing?

To test this assumption, we analyzed 12 feedback data sets, with results from thousands of people, to examine the competencies used to evaluate effectiveness. In our first test, we isolated the people perceived as having no strengths. (In previous studies, we concluded a "strength" is a competency rated at the 90th percentile or higher—

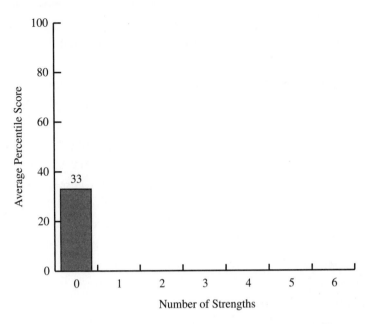

Figure 6.1 Perceived effectiveness of people with "no strengths."

much more than simply being "pretty good" at something. It is the ability to do something extraordinarily well.) We wondered what the overall effectiveness rating of a person would be if that person had no competencies rated as a strength. It turned out that those perceived as having no strengths were found, on average, to be at the 33rd percentile in overall perceived effectiveness (Figure 6.1).

The Impact of One Strength
We then isolated the people who had one competency rated at the 90th percentile or higher and calculated the overall perceived effectiveness for this group. Those perceived as

having one strength were found to be, on average, at the 57th percentile. To us, this was startling: Having one strength creates, on average, a 24-percentile point increase in overall perceived effectiveness—with the range being from 21 percent to 30 percent, depending on the competency models used.

This huge jump is difficult to explain: How does having one strength create such a dramatic effect on overall perceived effectiveness? Part of the answer seems to be the halo effect that comes from doing something well. When a person is highly competent in one area, people assume the person has strengths in other areas. A similar process works in the opposite way when a person has a major flaw (Figure 6.2).

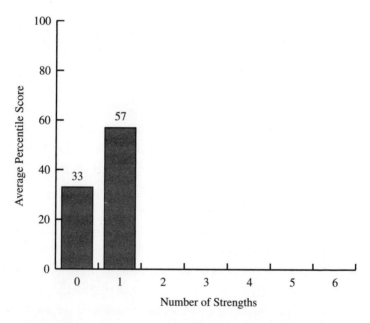

Figure 6.2   Impact of one strength on perceived effectiveness.

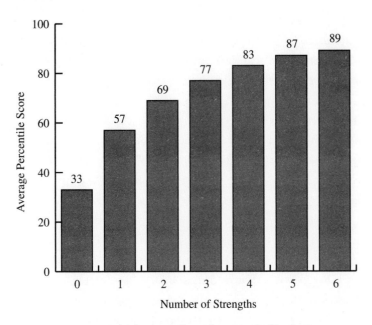

Figure 6.3   Multiple strengths and perceived effectiveness.

The Power of Multiple Strengths

Continuing our analysis, we isolated the people who had two or more competencies rated as strengths. On average, people with three strengths were found to be at the 77th percentile in overall perceived effectiveness (Figure 6.3).

Additional Studies on the Impact of Strengths

Although this study is very convincing on its own, the number of strengths is determined by assessing if a particular competency is at the 90th percentile. But a person's overall leadership effectiveness rating is the sum of all competencies averaged together. Using the same data to evaluate both strengths and overall effectiveness may cause cross correlations that could inflate the studies' outcome. To more accurately evaluate the impact of having strengths, an independent measure of leadership effectiveness should be used.

In another study, executives collected 360 assessments from managers, peers, and direct reports. The assessment included evaluations of 16 leadership competencies, a separate evaluation of the supervisory effectiveness of each manager, and a summary of employee satisfaction according to the direct reports of each manager (based on a 12-item index that assessed satisfaction with the company, individual job descriptions, the future of the company, career opportunities, and so forth). Each dataset was analyzed, and the number of strengths was determined for each manager. Figure 6.4 shows the results of this more balanced approach.

This study shows the impact of strengths on three different outcomes relating to perceived effectiveness. Although there appears to be a slight inflation in leadership effectiveness, the trend is consistent throughout the data. The study also illustrates the impact of strengths on employee satisfaction. In additional studies, we have found that leaders with strengths tended to be rated as more likely to be promoted, receive a greater number of stock options, and have direct reports who are less likely to quit. These studies demonstrate what we already intuitively knew: Doing something well has a substantial impact on overall perceived performance.

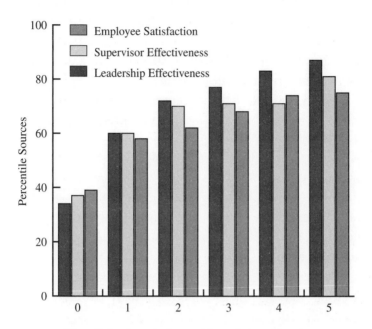

Figure 6.4   Impact of strength on three measures.

PRINCIPLE 24

Doing something well has a dramatic impact on perceived effectiveness.

The new research also brought out a few implications: First, although we tested multiple data sets, the results showed incredible consistency. The more data we analyzed, the more it confirmed our assumptions about the importance of building strengths. Second, it didn't seem to matter which competency people had strength in, as long as they performed that competency extremely well—at the 90th percentile or better. For me, this was the most significant implication, because there are some skills and competencies I may never perform extremely well. But I seem to have more natural talent and inherent motivation in other competencies. This suggests that people can choose which strength they want to build.

How to Build a Strength

How do you build a strength? Most people assume the way to build a strength is simply to do something faster, more frequently, or with greater endurance. But when people attempt to build a strength, they end up doing nothing, because they can't figure out how to improve any further.

Suppose you were creating an action plan for improving your technical expertise. A typical action plan might include actions such as taking a class, reading a book in the field, or going to a conference or seminar on the subject. These actions make a lot of sense if technical expertise is a weakness. But suppose your technical expertise is rated positively, and you want to develop it into a profound strength. Using the same actions would not be as helpful in this case, because the actions of taking classes, reading books, and attending seminars have, in essence, already been mastered. You've had the equivalent experience of these as you moved from poor to good in your performance and expertise.

In our research, Jack Zenger and I identified a new process for building strengths, that we called *nonlinear development*. We found that people who were the most effective in performing a particular competency also tended to be effective on a series of companion behaviors. These companion behaviors are similar to the ones presented in Chapter 3, which related to the ability to accept feedback. In theory, companion skills may be used to create an extremely high level of competence.

A similar approach is used in training athletes. If a typical runner with fair skills runs 20 miles per week, the runner could increase to 30 miles per week to become a better runner. But, to become a great runner, would it be wise to recommend that the person run 200 miles per week? Any runner or running coach would tell you that running 200 miles per week is risky, might cause more harm than good, and certainly invites injury. The way runners move from good to great is through cross training: They lift weights, swim, watch their diets, and do a variety of other things to build their strength.

In the same way, companion behaviors leverage your ability to perform a competency well and develop it into a profound strength.

7

Making Change Happen

The purpose of getting feedback, understanding it, and prioritizing the critical issues is to turn the feedback into change. Much has been written from many perspectives about how best to create personal change. However, different approaches work in different situations and with different people. So, rather than focus on one perspective, I present many different perspectives and approaches to change, and then you may use the approach that best fits your particular situation and personality.

Finding the Real Problem

Sometimes the root of the problem is not the obvious problem.

While reviewing the feedback she had received, Cheryl felt very confused. Her boss's feedback indicated that she did not involve others in decision making and problem solving. But the feedback she received from those who reported directly to her indicated that they felt highly involved.

Cheryl's first inclination was to involve her group even more in decisions. But, after discussing the issue with her boss, the real problem became clear: Her boss was the one left out of most decisions. Cheryl and her group had been making most of their decisions without involving the boss. With this insight, the problem switched to an issue of "how to manage her manager," rather than "how to manage her work group."

After people accept feedback, they tend to feel personally responsible for the resolution of problems. The first assumption they typically make is, "I need to change." The following example shows how making this assumption when a problem has no direct link to the person receiving the feedback can only add to frustrations.

Dick managed a group of engineers in a government laboratory. The feedback he received noted poor collaboration between his group of engineers and other groups. Dick recognized his competitive nature. He and his peers frequently argued over the resourcing of projects. He resolved to become more collaborative. He believed the problems existed because of his own competitive nature and because of some negative feelings he'd had about a few of his peers.

In reviewing his action plan, Dick made a list with two columns. The first column listed those peers with whom he'd had difficulty working collaboratively, and the other listed those with whom he could collaborate effectively. After making the two lists, Dick compared them. He found that all of the people with whom he'd had poor collaborative relationships were from the same organization. When asked why, he indicated that they worked in a matrix organization. His engineers provided a service very similar to what the top managers in the other organization had been trying to build internally.

"We argue about resources," he said, "because they use my people to finish jobs that they start but don't have the expertise to finish." But I think if I can just be more personable and not get hot-tempered, we can work these problems out.

However, the major reason Dick had problems with collaboration had little to do with his personality. It was a function of an organizational arrangement that placed one group in direct competition with another. For one year, Dick worked diligently to be a "nicer person." And, except for the fact that others noticed his willingness to "bend over backwards," new feedback measured no noticeable change in collaboration between the groups.

PRINCIPLE 25

A critical step in personal change is to change the strategies, structures, and systems that support or reinforce the behavior you desire to change.

To understand the organizational implications of your feedback, ask yourself these five questions:

1. How is this behavior rewarded by others in the organization?
2. Who encourages or discourages this behavior and why?
3. If I do this unwanted behavior, what good will happen? What bad will happen?
4. Is there something in the way this organization is designed and structured that reinforces this behavior?
5. Is there something within the systems (compensation, rewards, promotion, communications) of the organization that reinforces this behavior?

At one time in our consulting company we had a problem developing our associate consultants. They complained about how they always had to work on small, simple pieces of large projects, and how their development suffered because of it. In the meantime, our company rewarded its partners according to the amount of consulting revenue they generated. To optimize revenue, partners would only use associates on projects when they personally could not accomplish the work. In this way, partners' hours were almost fully billable, and their bonuses were very large.

Each of the partners recognized the importance of developing the associate consultants. We all wanted them to develop and become contributing members of the team. It was in our long-term best interests to develop them, but our individual behavior did not change—until we changed our compensation system. Once the new compensation system was in place, which rewarded partners for developing associate consultants, development began to occur. Under the new system, partners could make no more money, even if they did all the work themselves. Now, rather than try to do as much of the consulting as possible, partners tried to leverage the work of the associates.

In this example, our problem was to get partners to develop and coach new associates. Motivational speeches, reports, and sound logic may have changed the partners' behavior slightly, but changing the compensation system was what changed behavior substantially. The goal was to increase associates' involvement in projects. Changing the compensation system was what produced automatic behavior changes in the partners. Partners soon had the coaching and developing skills necessary to train associates, who could then ease the consulting loads of the partners. All the partners needed was a system that rewarded them for using associates.

Moving from General to Specific

Often, when we receive feedback, we generalize the feedback into a global expression of the problem. For example, we might say: "I need to communicate better," "I need to motivate and inspire others more," "I need to be more helpful and considerate," or "I need to deliver better results." Our research also shows that many people describe their change efforts in the same global terms. They might say, "I am going to improve my . . ." and end their sentence with an all-encompassing term: communications, motivation, consideration, performance, or results.

Gene Dalton, Louis Barnes, and Abraham Zaleznik explain that to change, people must adjust their change plans from general terms to specific. General plans or goals rarely lead to any actual change, and supply no specific actions to take. In fact, when you have a general goal for change, you cannot tell whether you are doing something about the goal or not. Specific plans set the goals in motion and provide detailed, specific actions that lead to goal accomplishment.[1] By keeping our change plans in general terms, we show that we never truly intend to change anything.

The following conversation I had with my son, about his grades in school, illustrates this idea:

> "Son, what are your goals for your grades in school next semester?"
>
> "I'm going to get better grades, Dad."
>
> "How much better?"
>
> "Oh, I don't know. But, you know, better than last semester."
>
> "Does that mean a straight-A average?"
>
> "No, not straight-As, Dad. But I'll do better. Can I go to Ben's house now?"
>
> "First, tell me your goal. How much better are your grades going to be?"
>
> "Just better, Dad. Why can't you just trust me to do better? Can I go to Ben's house now?"

By keeping the change goal general, my son did not have to commit to anything. General goals do not lead to any specific behaviors, such as studying for three hours per night, having homework done before any other activities, turning in all assignments, doing well on all tests, doing all extra credit assignments, and redoing any tests and assignments that resulted in lower grades. Therefore, the odds of achieving the goal are greatly reduced. General goals allow us to avoid the hassles of reality.

By creating specific goals, we force ourselves to consider what it will actually take to change. Part of the movement from general to specific goals is deciding what we will do. For example, you might set a general goal to be a better listener. But you will not take action until you set a more specific goal, specify action plans, and then measure your performance against those plans.

Your goals might be: "I will develop my listening skills so that my peers and those who report to me can communicate better with me, and so they will notice an improvement in my ability to understand and listen to them." Your action items might be the following:

1. I will stop all incoming phone calls when I am in a meeting by asking the receptionist to hold my calls. If an emergency phone call comes in, I will tell the person I am with that it is an emergency. If I expect an important call to come during a meeting, I will warn the person I am with that this may happen. At the next staff meeting, I will tell the staff that I have neglected to do these things until now. I will ask the staff to remind me whenever I deviate from these goals.

2. My peers and subordinates will know I understand their position. Whenever others tell me something, I will wait a few seconds and try to understand their point of view. I will restate their questions or comments in my own words, and ask if I have accurately

expressed their feelings. I will not interrupt while others are talking.

3 After giving assignments, I will ask others to summarize the instructions and repeat them to me. I will assure them that I only want to make sure I tell them everything they need to know to accomplish it.

Making general goals more specific can be difficult, because it forces you to make your goals actionable and measurable. When you create specific plans, make sure your smallest actions impact the overall goal. One way to do this is to review your action plan with another person, and test your plan to see if your plan makes the connection between your actions and goals.

Building a Support System

When responding to feedback, many people automatically assume they have to solve the problem themselves. As children, we were taught to clean up our own messes. As adults, we still assume a high degree of independence whenever we approach problems. Although it is wonderful that we feel a strong sense of personal responsibility for our behavior, I find that getting others involved in our change efforts greatly increases our chances of success.

Early in our organization's history, whenever a company would ask for a proposal from us, we would prepare the proposal, send it, and hope it addressed the company's needs and problems. Sometimes the proposal was right on, but other times it missed the mark completely.

We did not learn whether we hit or missed the mark until after we sent the proposal, or perhaps not until the company had made a decision to work with us or not.

After several years of this practice, one of our partners suggested that we prepare a draft of a proposal, send it to a member of the organization, and ask for some feedback. We tried this approach and, to our surprise, the internal person provided some great insights that helped us reframe our proposal and provide what the client needed. From then on, on all of our proposals, we would look for an internal "coach," and ask that coach for help and assistance. This proved to be an incredibly valuable tool.

If you were a parent and fearful that your teenager might be experimenting with drugs, what would be your first recommendation for making an effective change? The recommendation for change given by 95 percent of parents is to change the teen's peer group. Whenever teens experiment with drugs, they are probably not doing it alone.

We all know of the tremendous influence that peer groups can have on teens. Most adults assume that their own peer groups are much less influential because they are older. But the reality is that, as teens, we typically denied the extent to which we were influenced by our peers, and now we do the same thing as adults.

In an experiment described by Solomon Asch in his book, *Social Psychology,* people were asked for their perception of a situation. Others in the room had been told to disagree. The results showed that one-third of the people, both young and old, felt uncomfortable and changed perceptions.[2]

In their work on change in organizations, Gene Dalton, Louis Barnes, and Abraham Zaleznik note the importance of "altering old relationships and establishing new social ties" as an important aspect of successful change efforts.[3] Asking others for assistance helps you in two ways: First, it alters the relationships you have with people who may have been rewarding the behaviors you wish to change, because you are asking those people to help you stop or start a particular behavior. Second, by asking people who are good at a behavior for their help, you begin new relationships with people who will reward your new behavior.

We typically do not ask others for assistance for three reasons, which are myths:

Myth 1. Asking Others for Help Is a Strong Admission That You Have a Problem. For example, I like to set New Year's resolutions, but I do not tell anyone. That makes it easier to forget them. As soon as I tell people about my resolutions, they remind me when I forget.

Other problems can be more embarrassing. For example, in a corporate structure where others have influence over new jobs and promotions, most people feel it would be politically unwise to ask others for help. But, although some people might use this against you, most people are favorably impressed at your willingness to ask for help.

Do not assume your problems are a big secret. Most people already know, and asking them for help causes them to change their perceptions and think of you in a new light.

Myth 2. Asking for Help Is a Sign of Weakness and Highlights Your Inability to Solve the Problem Yourself. As long as you believe this, you will not ask for help. When people ask me for help, I am very impressed by their forthrightness. Done in a positive way, asking for help signals confidence, strength of commitment, and a willingness to learn from mistakes.

Myth 3. Others Do Not Want to Be Bothered; Asking for Their Help Imposes on Their Time. Although sometimes this is true, you can always ask in a way that will allow others to tell you they are busy and do not have the time. Most often, when you ask others for help, they are flattered that you have asked them.

One of the most positive experiences you can have is helping, teaching, or mentoring others. Reflect back on when you taught your children to ride a bike, play ball, or ski. Most people feel as positive about those experiences as those who learned the skill. Helping others is intrinsically rewarding, and most of us are happy to do it.

Watching Those Who Are Good

Much of successful management, leadership, and interpersonal effectiveness is more of an art than a science. Much of it is subtle and elusive. Learning these skills is like learning to ride a bike: You can read about it, watch others do it, and study all the laws, but ultimately, if you want to learn, you have to try. But, your attempts will be more successful if you carefully watch someone else ride a bike first. Although it is possible to learn on your own, watching people who do things well and mimicking their behaviors will help you learn faster.

Jeff was staring into space as the facilitator approached him during a training session designed to help people create action plans based on the feedback they had received.

"How are you doing?" asked the facilitator, trying to sound encouraging.

"I have no idea what I can do to solve this issue. You asked us to develop specific behavioral action plans. And, although I understand the issue and can write a goal, I can't think specifically about what I will do."

His goal statement read, "Think and act more strategically." The facilitator asked Jeff if he knew of anyone in the organization who did this well.

"Yes," he replied, "Bill is recognized as the best strategic thinker in the company."

After talking for a minute about Bill and his abilities, the facilitator suggested that Jeff do two things: "First, ask Bill for some help; and second, watch and study what Bill does. After that, you can begin to write specific behaviors on your action plan."

One factor that can have a major influence on success in a career is the job assignment. New assignments offer people the chance to experience new and different situations that can help them learn and grow. It also introduces them to other people who can teach them, and who will coach and counsel them.

PRINCIPLE 26

Close observation of others who have demonstrated skills will help you develop the same skills.

Observing how others interact, react, present, think, and decide is extremely valuable. Developing good observation skills is essential for learning. Many people who are part of a situation do not watch closely, and often miss some of the more subtle techniques. Anyone can learn from the obvious, but few people are careful enough to watch and learn the subtle skills needed to move up in the organization.

Early in my career, a young associate and I were assigned to present a proposal to a prospective client we had never met. We arrived a few minutes early, so I started a brief conversation to get to know the client better. We had a pleasant discussion for about 10 minutes, and then my companion presented our proposal. After the meeting, my companion and I were walking to the car when he said, "How do you do that?"

"Do what?" I replied.

"Small talk. You didn't know anything about that person, but within 10 minutes you got acquainted, got to know about her background, found several similar interests, and had a few laughs. I can't do that," he said, "and I wish I could."

But he was a great observer. This happened early in his career, and several years later I observed him again, and found that he had developed this skill very well.

Astute observation is a skill many people lack. We sit in a meeting, thinking we are accurately observing what is happening, but we still miss so much. We get so caught up in our own conversations, or in making our own points, that we miss much of what actually transpires. Carefully watching those who are skillful can be a critical part of learning a new skill.

Making Your Own Mental Video

Pat received some direct and highly negative feedback about her temper. Even though she did not lose her temper every day, she had "lost it" several times during the past year. The feedback had not been unexpected. Although she recognized this had been a problem for some time, it seemed to her that whenever she lost her temper it always helped her get the results she wanted quickly.

"I don't plan to lose my temper," she said. "I'm on autopilot, and it just happens. I guess I don't control it very well. I feel bad every time it happens, but it just keeps happening."

Pat's goal was clear, and the behavior was measurable and well defined. But she remained at a loss about how to change. "Trying harder doesn't seem to help," she admitted.

The facilitator discussed with Pat an approach to changing her temper problem. The first thing Pat needed was to develop the skill to recognize her anger prior to "losing it." In the past, she had always tried to control herself after she got very angry, but she would only find herself on autopilot. The facilitator pointed out that, for most people, once they become really angry the adrenaline takes over, and they can maintain little control over their actions. The key to controlling anger is to catch yourself in the initial stages of frustration, when there is still a high level of personal control. After going back through several specific incidents, Pat started to recognize the preliminary signs of anger.

The second step involved Pat walking herself through past bad temper scenarios, recognizing the warning signs, and imagining herself working through the scenarios in positive ways. She imagined herself recognizing the warning signs and then asking that she be excused to go to the restroom. She also imagined herself dealing with people in ways that would not fire up her anger. She passed through these imaginary scenarios in graphic detail and repeated each of them several times with different variations.

Computers cannot calculate correct answers until someone programs them. Even though computers have the capacity to calculate correct answers, nothing can happen until a program is invoked to execute that capacity. In the same way, we all need to be programmed. You need to create your own internal action movie and rehearse your part. You cannot just make up your mind to behave differently in a given situation and expect to succeed, without first having a rich sense of what that new behavior looks like, how you will react, and what you will say.

Mental movies begin with observations and research. Determine what the correct behavior looks like. Then play it out in your mind. To do this well, you must use your imagination—your visualizations should reach a high level of detail. For example, if I had to deal with my temper, I might ask myself: "What is a situation in which I am easily provoked? When I am provoked, how do my stomach and chest feel? What is my heart rate? Am I blushing? What am I thinking? How does my face look? What are my hands doing? What is my posture? If I am sitting, am I sitting back in my chair, or on the edge of the chair?" I need to imagine how I look, feel, and act, and then try to recreate those emotions.

Next, start to imagine how you will change your behavior. Recognize that you are beginning to become angry. Play out the recognition process. Imagine yourself being proud of recognizing the problem before you lose control.

Now systematically start to turn off all the physical symptoms: Your heart rate goes down. You are no longer blushing. Your hands are relaxed. You sit back in your seat. Your face is relaxed. You begin to smile. You adjust your thinking: "This guy is not trying to make me look stupid; he is just trying to make himself look good."

By imagining detail, people often find that they do not always know what the appropriate behavior looks like. This usually encourages them to go back and study or observe. Visualization is a valuable tool that allows us to plan our behaviors before we act.

Most of our behaviors each day come in reaction to situations, instead of through calculation and careful thought. When we first learn a new skill, such as golf or tennis, we must think through almost every move (e.g., pull the club back, look at the ball, bring the club forward swiftly, and hit the ball). But, once we have mastered the skill, rather than rationally thinking through every move we make and every word we say, our actions become second nature.

Like an announcer at a sports event, however, we constantly observe our own behavior: "What a stupid thing to say." "That was brilliant!" or, "Be careful, this could be tricky." The internal commentary runs freely, but many times our "commentator" within cannot get us to perform perfectly.

In his book, *The Inner Game of Tennis,* W. Timothy Gallwey discusses the effects of this inner dialogue.[4] As commentator, you make judgments about yourself. All of your judgments are subjective evaluations of events. For example, you might say: "I am making a good impression." "I think she likes me." "They think I am an idiot." or, "He thinks I don't know what I am talking about." And, since you trust our own commentary, you do not view these evaluations as subjective, but rather as highly objective.

Internally, you also have an actor. The actor is the part of you that executes behaviors, whereas the commentator within makes judgments and tells the actor what to do. However, the actor does not always act the way the commentator wants. The actor is like a computer. Once the actor has learned something (is programmed), he generally repeats the action. But the commentator can significantly influence the actor.

Gallwey contrasts the typical approach to learning with the inside approach. Here is the typical approach:

- *Step One:* You make subjective evaluations about your behavior: "I have got to stop cutting people off in discussions. It makes me seem too authoritarian."
- *Step Two:* You decide to change, and you verbally tell yourself what you need to do to change: "All right now, just sit back and listen. Make sure the person is through talking before you speak. In fact, count to 10 before you speak."
- *Step Three:* You work hard to make this happen and force yourself to do it right: "Watch closely for when that person is finished. Do not jump in. Do not jump the gun; wait; wait. Now talk."
- *Step Four:* You make subjective evaluations about the results and try again: "Oh, I blew it again. I have to watch myself and force myself to change."

Now let's consider some steps for how to apply Gallwey's "Inner Way":

- *Step One:* You observe your behavior in a descriptive way: "I am cutting people off before they have finished speaking."
- *Step Two:* You decide to change, and visualize what the change would look like and how you would feel: "I do not always cut people off in conversations. What do I do differently when I cut people off and

when I do not? I will observe myself in different conversations and figure out what the difference is.

"After observation, I find that I often cut people off when I am in a hurry, when I do not think the other person is very smart and does not have good ideas, or when I really want to prove my point. I also have a better sense for how I feel when it happens, how I sit in my chair, and what I focus on when I do not cut people off. I have also learned what my face does differently in the two situations. I have created in my mind a very clear picture of the different behaviors."

- *Step Three:* You relax and try to execute your vision. Rather than simply trying harder, make your behavior look like the vision in your head.
- *Step Four:* You objectively review what happened and try again.

Whether you succeed or fail, try to remain objective about what happened. Try again and again, so that in the future your behavior will be more automatic.

Defining Feedback Positively

When we receive negative feedback, we tend to deny that we have failed. Since the feedback comes from others, by accepting negative feedback at face value we feel that others are in control—a common cause of frustration. By redefining negative feedback, making it positive, we can accept their feedback and apply it to improve our motivation to change.

PRINCIPLE 27

Redefining negative feedback in a positive light creates increased motivation to change.

In their book, *When Smart People Fail,* Carole Hyatt and Linda Gottlieb discuss the problems some successful people have when they encounter failure.[5] When failure makes us feel powerless and like a victim, change does not occur. They recommend you reinterpret your story by casting your feedback in a more positive light, one in which you have more control.

Jerry was a hard-driving, energetic manager in a high-tech manufacturing environment. The feedback he had received, for the most part, had been positive, but one area was very negative: "Jerry is the most sarcastic person I have ever met," read one comment.

Jerry agreed and said, "I love to be sarcastic. I live to be sarcastic. That's how I survive around here. If I can't be sarcastic and irreverent, I don't think I can work here."

No thing or person was insulated from Jerry's sarcasm. He frequently included his boss, the president of the company, in his sarcasm, along with many other people. For him, this was all in good fun and did not mean anything. But not everyone was sure Jerry was joking. Those who reported to Jerry often became outspoken and negative about company programs after they had heard Jerry rip them apart. Still, Jerry did not want to give up his sarcasm, and he did not like the fact that others seemed to be pressuring him to do so. Jerry wrestled with this issue for several weeks. He contended that sarcasm did not hurt anyone. The facilitator asked him to talk to several people openly about his sarcasm. After a few weeks Jerry reinterpreted his story:

> When I was an entry-level engineer, nobody listened to my sarcasm or gave it much credence. Then I moved fast into management positions, but I didn't think people saw me any differently than when I had been an entry-level engineer. As hard as it is for me to believe, I know that people at lower levels look to me like I know something. I had never realized I had that kind of influence, or that my sarcasm affected attitudes and morale the way it did. I suppose getting the negative feedback on sarcasm is a compliment: It means that people perceive me to have a fair amount of influence.

After Jerry reinterpreted his story and regained control, his willingness to change improved significantly. The original feedback made him feel that something was being taken from him, that others were forcing him to change. He rationalized his bad habit as "not a problem" because of his sense of failure and lack of control. By reframing the feedback, he did not see that he had to change his personality at all, but the reframing did create the motivation he needed to modify his behavior.

When we interpret negative feedback as failure, we find it difficult to change. By reinterpreting feedback, we take the feedback and recast it in a positive light that encourages change. One caution: Make sure your reinterpreting does not become rationalization.

Looking Out for Labels

All of us have labels that define who we are. For example, you might label yourself as: "I am an engineer," "I am quiet," "I am organized," or "I am competitive." Sometimes feedback confronts the labels that people give themselves:

Vickie received feedback that told her she needed to better communicate with others in the office. "I am just quiet," she said. "That's the problem, and I can't change that."

Derrick was told he needed to improve his presentation skills. He responded, "I'm an engineer, not a salesman."

Some labels motivate and inspire you to achieve goals, but others serve as a ball and chain, causing you to resist progress. If your change goals confront preexisting labels, you may need to give up some of the old labels and take on some new ones. Often, however, people resist giving up these labels. The labels, even though unproductive, provide them with security and a way of defining who they are as well as who they are not.

Vickie confronted her label and modified it from "I'm quiet" to "I'm a quiet communicator: A person doesn't have to be loud and boisterous to communicate, but they do have to send messages. I found I needed to take the initiative to let others know what I was doing and what I needed from them."

Most of the time, Vickie uses memos, e-mail, or brief conversations in the hall. Others still think Vickie is quiet, but now they know what she is doing.

Derrick, a very competent engineer, used his label to hide from his fear of talking in front of groups: "I can't talk in front of other people. I'm just not good at it."

"How many times have you done it?" asked the facilitator.

"Once or twice," he admitted.

"Have you ever been good at something you haven't practiced?"

Derrick eventually agreed to practice and see what would happen. He took a public speaking course and joined Toastmasters. With practice, Derrick soon turned into an excellent presenter.

Try It—You'll Like It (After a While)

After working with many people who have tried to change their eating habits, I have reached the conclusion that people like what they frequently eat. Whenever I have asked a person to eat foods that are different from the foods they usually eat, the conversation usually goes something like this:

"I don't like that kind of food."

"I know you don't like it, and the reason you don't like it is because you don't eat it," I reply.

"Oh no, you don't understand. The reason I don't eat it is because I don't like it," they insist.

"I understand you perfectly. Please believe me when I say that the reason you don't like those foods is because you don't eat them."

Most people believe they have chosen what foods they like or dislike. It's as if their taste buds have a mind of their own, or that some mystical force has caused them to like some foods and dislike others. People even characterize themselves as having personalities linked to the foods they eat: "I'm a meat-and-potatoes person," or "I'm not the salad-bar type." But I have found that if you eat a particular food often enough, even though you mildly dislike it when you begin to eat it, you will eventually begin to like that food, and perhaps even crave it.

You have probably tasted foods from foreign countries and had negative reactions. I still remember my first taste of Korean *kimchi*. My next-door neighbor was from Korea, and while visiting one day, she offered me a taste of *kimchi*. I though it was terrible. I immediately wondered what genetic mishap had occurred in the Korean people that would have caused them to actually like pickled cabbage.

The next day I went to McDonald's and bought a Big Mac. I asked my Korean neighbor to take a bite and tell me what she thought. She told me she did not like it. I asked her not to hold back and to tell me what she really thought of it. She replied, "It's terrible." That had been my exact reaction to *kimchi*.

That had also been my first reaction to Perrier water. After my first glass, I remember saying to myself, "I don't get it; I thought this was supposed to be good." I probably would not have ever tasted Perrier water again, but one day, while traveling on an airplane, I decided I wanted to find a substitute for all the soft drinks I consumed. With few choices available that day, I tried Perrier with a twist of lime. I concluded that it was slightly better than water. I continued to drink Perrier on every flight. After about a month of flying every week, I even started to crave Perrier. I have tried the same process with many foods. I am convinced that anybody can like any reasonable food if they will eat it often enough to develop a taste for it.

PRINCIPLE 28

Those things we persist in doing eventually change our feelings and appetites.

Changing our habits is often like changing what we eat. At first we do not like it, or it doesn't feel natural. But those things we persist in doing eventually change our feelings and appetites. What was not satisfying and fulfilling in the past can become satisfying and fulfilling in the future, if we persist.

People often limit their abilities to make changes because they believe their personal characteristics, tastes, and habits define who they are and what they like. Beginning from the time you accepted such ideas, you may have developed elaborate rationalizations that support and reinforce these habits: "I am the way I am, because that is the way I like to be," "This is the way God made me," or "Various circumstances created my personal characteristics, traits, and habits, and if those circumstances were different, I would also be different."

To make ourselves more comfortable with who we are and what we do, we often rationalize our interests, thinking that "this is just the way we are supposed to be," "this is just what we like," or dislike, feel, think, or hate. This is why people act as victims. They have not designed their own character—it has been designed for them by circumstances. We can simply accept ourselves the way we are, or we can choose to change the way we are and design the new person we want to be. Although we cannot change our circumstances, we can change how we choose to respond to them.

For example, if you like high-fat foods, you can choose to eat other foods. It is not very likely that your love for high-fat foods will disappear overnight. In fact, it may never leave you, but over time, you will develop a passion for other foods. If you are authoritarian, angry, argumentative, insensitive, dismissive, pompous, overly analytical, or a pushover, you can change. But you have to decide to act differently. Of course, you will find resistance to change, because you have taken many years to build up a great rationale for why it is good to be the way you are and why those who are different from you are of less value.

At first your actions will seem foreign. You will not feel comfortable with how you are acting. You will not be as effective for a while, but if you persist, over time you will begin to love your new behaviors. You will feel comfortable. The behaviors will feel natural, normal, and appropriate. You will be even more effective and happy than you were before, and you will recognize that you can influence your situation.

Trapped by Beliefs

Sometimes we can get trapped by our beliefs, as the following example attests.

Maria's feedback suggested that she rarely recognized or rewarded those who reported to her. The facilitator asked her if she felt the feedback was accurate.

She said, "I'm not one of those managers that praises people every time they show up for work on time, but I think I'm fair. I think my people get all the praise they need."

The facilitator then asked how much recognition and praise she felt people needed.

"Not much. People just need to be responsible and do their job. You do your job because it's what you are supposed to do, and you shouldn't have to be praised for every accomplishment. It's just part of your job."

The facilitator then asked Maria to talk about when she was a child, growing up: "How did your parents feel about praise and recognition?"

"They thought children should do their work because it's the right thing to do. They never had to praise me or tell me how wonderful I was, but I knew they were proud of me. They had high expectations, and I fulfilled their expectations."

The facilitator asked if she thought others had been raised with similar expectations and parents who rarely praised. She assumed that most had not been: "My husband's parents were almost the opposite. They praised my husband for everything. My husband wishes I would praise our children more."

As Maria explored her belief system, she found that she considered too much praise to be bad. She believed praise robbed people of the chance to accomplish tasks on their own. No wonder she had a difficult time praising others. Although she had set many goals, such as creating praising timetables, nothing worked until she critically examined her belief system and changed her core beliefs.

In their book, *Prisoners of Belief,* Matthew McKay and Patrick Fanning indicate that core beliefs "define how you feel about yourself and the emotional tone of your life."[6] Our beliefs include our feelings about our competence and abilities, attitudes about other people, stereotypes, values, and motives. Beliefs such as Maria's are maintained by a process called "selective attention"—only paying attention to events that support a belief system and ignoring those that do not. McKay and Fanning call this "mental grooving," falling into a rut that makes it easier to deal with situations and people. We can break free from some of these self-defeating beliefs by first understanding our core beliefs and the rules associated with such beliefs. One of Maria's rules was "praising people destroys individual responsibility."

PRINCIPLE 29

Changing behavior often requires changing core beliefs.

We can also go through the process of testing our beliefs in an objective way. When we test our beliefs, we often recognize that our rigid personal rules are not true. In Maria's case, she found that recognition and praise could actually build individual responsibility.

Finally, we can develop new beliefs that support and reinforce positive behavior. There is a psychological disorder called "imagined ugliness" (body dimorphic disorder). People imagine they are ugly when they are not. These people focus extensively on small defects and exaggerate them: "My hands and fingers do not look right." They focus all their attention on small, irrelevant things. Therapy to help these individuals focuses on teaching them to be more objective and realistic in their evaluations.

As you consider changing some of your behaviors, ask yourself: "What beliefs, values, or rules do I have that support and reinforce the behavior I am attempting to change?" Sometimes, to change your behavior, you have to change your beliefs.

Goals and Behavior Shaping

Sometimes we hope to acquire or change behaviors that are quite complex. They may not be things we can currently do. For example, you may want to become a more confident and comfortable public speaker, but it may be a very difficult skill for you to acquire. If you cannot currently do the skill exactly as you wish, you may find it difficult to begin the change process. This is when shaping becomes helpful.

I first encountered shaping in an animal behavior class in college. I was assigned to train a rat to press a lever to get water. The animals had been deprived of water and then placed in the cage with the lever. I waited patiently for the rat to press the lever, but it never went close to the lever. By the end of the lab period, the rat was still thirsty, and it had made no attempt to press the lever. I felt very discouraged.

Then I learned about behavior shaping. In behavior shaping, you reward successive approximations of a desired behavior. During the next lab period, I began by giving the rat a drink as soon as it turned toward the lever. Though turning toward the lever was not the final desired result, I could reward this approximate behavior since I could not train the rat to push the lever until it learned where the lever was. Soon the rat began to quickly turn toward the lever each time. Then I waited for the rat to turn and also approach the lever before I rewarded it. I was amazed at how fast the shaping process worked. By the end of the second session, the rat busily pressed the lever whenever it wanted water.

Although the behaviors we try to change are much more complex, the same principle works. Reward successive approximations of the desired behavior.

PRINCIPLE 30

Rewarding successive approximations of a desired new behavior increases the likelihood of acquiring the new behavior.

To be a confident and comfortable public speaker, you might begin by making short comments in front of other people. In a staff meeting or at a lunch in a discussion with peers, make comments and express your opinion. Although what you are doing is not public speaking, it is the beginning step. As you become more comfortable, increase the steps and try something harder. Lay out a plan of successive steps that will help you accomplish your goals. Then, during the shaping process, do not forget your ultimate goal of performing a desired behavior.

When Jim learned from his feedback that others felt he "didn't think strategically," he admitted that he had "a difficult time trying to get his arms around the issue."

"I don't know how to start thinking strategically," he said. "I agree with the feedback, but I don't know how to change."

Jim met with the facilitator and outlined an action plan that would begin with reading and study. Next, he was to have a meeting with his boss to discuss the issue and ask for advice and coaching. Third, he was to attend a course on strategic thinking. Fourth, he would have a series of informal discussions with his peers about the rationale for the current strategy and direction of the company. The fifth step was for Jim to identify one other person recognized as an excellent strategic thinker; then he would look for opportunities to work with that person and ask him or her to be a mentor.

After all this, Jim was to write a white paper on the strategy of his company and the actions his department could take that would support and enhance the company strategy. He was to share the paper first with his boss, asking for feedback, and then with his peers and mentor.

After designing this action plan, Jim said, "Now at least I can make some progress toward my goal."

Rewarding Yourself

To encourage my four-year-old son to eat his dinner, I often would hold out the dessert as a reward. It seemed to work quite well. Most adults agree that rewards are very motivating for children, but they often do not know how to use rewards to motivate themselves in a change process. As you look over your goals for change, consider giving yourself rewards for achieving interim goals in the plan. The reward should be related to the changing behavior. For example, "When I lose 15 pounds on this diet, I will go out and buy myself some attractive new clothing." The nice thing about this reward is that it is related to the change process.

Your reward does not always have to be related to what you are trying to change. For example: "If I go three months without losing my temper, I will take a day of vacation, just for me." Or, "Whenever I listen without interrupting, I get to have a piece of my favorite candy." The value of these rewards should not be so high that you work only to get the rewards, but your rewards should symbolize accomplishment. The process of setting up contingencies for rewards will help you see progress toward your goals.

Building Self-Esteem

In their research on change, Gene Dalton, Louis Barnes, and Abraham Zaleznik found that, for people to continue to change, they need to have positive feelings about themselves. Often, as we begin to change, we find ourselves in embarrassing or difficult situations. These situations sometimes lead us to have more negative self-esteem.[7]

When Debbie received the feedback that she was "too bossy," she agreed with the feedback and became very serious about changing herself. She made her first attempt to change during her next department meeting. Rather than controlling the conversation and making all the decisions, Debbie determined to be "just another member of the group."

After the meeting, the facilitator asked Debbie how things went. "Terrible," she replied. "That was the worst meeting I ever attended. When I was bossy, at least something got done. Now my people think I am also stupid."

Debbie's optimistic hopes ended up in disaster. Later, several people in the meeting told her it would have been better if she had been "bossy." At that point, she felt that she would be safer by reverting back to her old behavior than to try something she was not very good at. She felt like a failure.

If we have the option, we will not continue to do things that make us look stupid. To continue changing, you need to build your self-esteem. Damaged self-esteem may help you recognize the need for change, but if the negative, self-defeating experiences continue, you will do whatever it takes to return to a more normal state and a more positive situation. Even though long-term change would be good for you, the negative short-term impact of the attempt can abort any progress and kill the attempt.

Some people can take more abuse than others. Some can even encounter several negative experiences in a row and not give up. But, if negative, ego-damaging experiences continue, everyone eventually gives up.

In planning for change, most of us underestimate the impact of negative experiences. Because of this, our attempts to change must provide support as well as challenge. Debbie's change plan needed to be more gradual. Not only had she entered her meeting unprepared, but others in the meeting were unaware of her efforts and lacked the skills necessary to help her succeed. Her change plan could only succeed through an abundance of peer support and an occasional challenge.

More on Codependence

In Chapter 4, I presented the concept of codependence in the treatment of alcoholism. The term *codependence* describes the relationship between the alcoholic and those close to the alcoholic whose behaviors support and reinforce the drinking problem. The codependents never outwardly support and reinforce the drinking. Instead, they support and reinforce other behaviors that cause the alcoholic to want to drink.

I sometimes lose my temper with my children. I desperately want to change. I work on my own behavior and try to control my emotions. Just when I start to feel that I am doing well, my teenage son and I may have a confrontation. I am under control, but he knows how to get to me. I persist, but so does my son. Finally, I break and lose my temper. Who has the problem? Is it me, my son, or both of us?

I almost never lost my temper before I had a teenager, but I cannot blame my lack of control on him. The answer to "Who has a problem?" is that we both have a problem. The solution is that we both need to change. I need to practice control, and he needs to understand what makes me angry. By involving my son in my change efforts, I improve my chances of change.

In most interpersonal issues, you can find codependents that can influence the ability to change. And, although it is possible to change without involving others, your chances of success increase significantly when you involve others. To involve others in your change efforts, you first need to understand the nature of your codependence: "When I act in a dismissive way toward my administrative assistant, it is typically when she has not finished my work on time."

The next step is to ask your codependent for help, instead of assigning blame. Your codependent needs to be just as committed to change as you are.

Third, you need to engage in honest, open discussion regarding the nature of the codependence: "Whenever you do such and such, I respond by doing this. I would like to change this behavior. Will you help me?"

At this point in the process, you may want to involve a third party who will help you see the impact of your own behaviors. You do not want to transfer the problem in your behavior to the behavior of others, such as by saying: "The only reason I act the way I do is because you act the way you do. Therefore, this is not my problem; it is your problem."

PRINCIPLE 31

*For many changes, you can increase the likeli-
hood of positive change by persuading others to
change with you.*

The most frequent comment I hear in these change ini-
tiatives is: "I cannot change until my boss changes." By
making your success or failure dependent on the hope
that others may change, you create a sure formula for
failure. Just because codependence exists and others influence you does not invalidate your ability to cope and
to change. The key is not to get others to change, but
first to become personally committed to the change, and
then ask others for help in changing with you.

One paradox about personal change is that people
who recommend change often also resist the change:

David received feedback that those who reported to him
wanted more involvement and participation in decisions. He
created an effective action plan to make changes. But, after
several months, he reported, "The very people who asked for
change seem to be resisting change. It seems that they
wanted to be involved in all the fun decisions, but not the difficult or complex ones."

Because changes in you will affect others, as changes
begin to occur, others will react either positively or negatively to your change. The key to having others support
your change is to ask them for their assistance in your
change and for their commitment to also change.

How to Avoid Feeling Deprived

What is the difference between moving to a new home because you have just won a new home in a sweep-stakes, and moving to another home because you have just declared bankruptcy? It is obvious which one you would prefer. Although either would require you to move, you would be excited about winning a sweep-stakes but depressed about going bankrupt.

Whenever we attempt to change, we often focus too much attention on what we cannot do, or on what we are losing, rather than on what we are gaining. When this occurs, our change attempts fail. Whenever we deny our-selves something we want, we feel deprived. As long as we feel deprived, we run the risk of succumbing to our base desires in the future. Often, these feelings of depri-vation come because we tell ourselves we cannot have something. The more we tell ourselves we cannot have something, the more we want it, and the stronger the feelings of deprivation become. Such vicious cycles often happen with diets. Long-term success in weight loss is seldom determined by your level of self-discipline in not eating certain foods. If your diet requires a lot of self-discipline, sooner or later you give up. It takes too much work, too much effort, and too much attention. High ef-fort can be maintained for some time, but eventually we all need to rest.

I believe change does have something to do with dili-gence and effort, but it has more to do with creating new desires, attitudes, passions, and emotions. If you can change your desires, you will not feel deprived. You then can do whatever you want to do, eat whatever you want to eat, without having to force yourself to do something you don't want to do.

BAD EXAMPLE: "I really want that cake, but I will force myself to eat the fruit plate instead."
GOOD EXAMPLE: "That cake looks very rich. I do not like that much sugar, and I know I will not feel good after I eat it. I think I will choose the fruit plate instead; it looks very good."

Although it may be true that you cannot talk yourself into different desires, by focusing your attention on what you cannot have, you crave it all the more. The key to avoiding feelings of deprivation is to focus on the benefits of the change, rather than on the loss caused by change. Paying constant attention to what we are giving up only makes us feel more deprived. It is often difficult not to focus on the loss. You need to remind yourself that you can have or do anything you want, but you have chosen not to. No one is forcing you.

Change Requires Practice

We would never consider coaching an athletic team without scheduling time to practice. But most of us have little practice time or coaching experience. To most of us it is all execution, but for others there is a strong sense that "you cannot make a mistake," and they feel so much pressure that they find it very difficult to try new behaviors.

Edward received feedback that told him he "did not deal well with conflict." This did not come as a surprise to him. He felt his chest tighten whenever he became involved in conflict situations, and, because of this, he usually avoided dealing with conflict. Whenever conflicts would arise, he would either get someone else to deal with it, avoid it, or write his infamous memos. But he knew that his future success would depend on developing the ability to handle conflicts.

"I know what to do," he said. "I've seen others do it well. I know I can do it, and I would rather avoid than confront." He became determined to solve his problem, and the next day, when a conflict situation arose, he jumped in with both feet.

Later, when he reviewed the situation, he remarked, "Now I know why I avoid conflict. It was a disaster. I thought I knew what to do, but that guy blew me away. My administrative assistant handles conflict better than I do."

Edward wanted to change, but he did not take the time to practice. No one would ever recommend playing professional football or performing a piano concerto in front of a large audience without first getting in shape and practicing.

Edward had confronted a "professional conflict user" who was very good at what he did. Edward first needed to get in shape and practice before taking on a "pro." He also needed to ask for help: "I'm not very good at dealing with conflict, but I'm trying to improve, so help me out here."

Sometimes practicing change is fairly straightforward. At other times, we may not know how to practice. Here are some practice tips:

- ▣ Read an article or book.
- ▣ Attend a training course.
- ▣ Listen to an audiotape.

- Ask your spouse or a close friend to help you practice at home. Role play different situations.
- Watch people who are very good at the behavior, and try to model your behavior after theirs.
- Ask someone who is very good to be your coach or mentor.
- Acknowledge your weakness in the situation and ask others for help.
- Develop a rich "internal videotape" of what you will do in different situations.
- Look for off-line opportunities to practice. For example, if you are trying to improve your abilities as a coach or mentor, ask if you could coach a little league baseball team.
- Try out new things on your spouse, children, or friends. (Let them know you are trying out and practicing some new behaviors before you surprise them.)
- Look for chances to work on a team with others who do this behavior well.
- Practice the behavior in a church, civic, or community setting.
- Take a temporary assignment that will allow you to practice the new behavior.

The Art of the Trade-Off

The difficult part about selecting just a few issues to work on is that it requires us to make trade-offs. Ours is not a society of trade-offs. Our society wants it all and is used to having it all. We want careers, close interpersonal relationships, adventure, and leisure. We want security and freedom. We want to make a lot of money, but we do not want to spend a lot of time at work.

Most people feel that successful people go through life and accomplish incredible feats almost effortlessly. We also see role models who seem to have it all. But nobody has it all. Every person who has achieved success in one area has been forced to make trade-offs in other areas of their life. To get something, you have to give something up.

Sue's feedback indicated that those who reported to her requested more frequent feedback and coaching. She realized this would require a lot of time. She knew she had the skills required to provide more feedback and coaching. But, ultimately, making this change would boil down to her willingness to trade some of her time from her direct involvement in project details for providing more feedback and coaching to her staff.

Sue did not find it difficult to provide direct and frequent feedback. In fact, she had become quite good at providing feedback and coaching in thoughtful and sensitive ways. However, she did find it more difficult to manage her time tightly. She liked to come to the office and take her time to accomplish paperwork and other administrative tasks. She did not like to hurry through paperwork or rush tasks. She felt a greater sense of accomplishment from finishing the administrative work than from the feedback and coaching.

The difficulty in making this change for Sue was that she needed to choose between the desire of others to receive more feedback and coaching from her, and her desire to take more time on administrative work.

As we make changes, we need to be clear about what we will lose in exchange for what we will gain. When we first try to change, we want to do it, and we see some of the obvious trade-offs. However, we often fail to see that change sometimes requires additional trade-offs. These other trade-offs are more difficult, because they are not expected. For example, the alcoholic trying to give up drinking does not want to stop going to the pub every night to see his friends. Although it is possible to give up drinking and still go to the pub, it is even more likely that after a short time the alcoholic will start drinking again if he continues to go to the pub.

An old Chinese proverb says: "The man who chases two rabbits loses them both." Making trade-offs can create great power in the change process, whereas not making trade-offs may substantially reduce a person's chance of making significant change.

Enjoying the Process

Ultimately, we persist in doing the things we most enjoy. We can make temporary changes or adaptations, but in the final analysis, the things that stick to us are the things we enjoy. The paradox of this principle is that if we persist in doing something, we can change from forced or difficult behaviors to automatic behaviors that become enjoyable.

Barry was told that he was not "people-oriented." He was very skilled in quickly picking up a seemingly endless variety of techniques that would help accomplish his tasks.

At first, others were impressed with the variety of changes in technique, but after a few months the novelty began to wear off among those who worked in Barry's group. Barry admitted the problem was he "didn't like those people. They were so mediocre and unmotivated. They all seemed satisfied just staying where they were, and I didn't want to start thinking the way they did."

However, Barry realized that, until he could get his group to support and trust him, he would not get promoted either: "I gave up on the techniques and just started to get to know the people. It took a few months, but finally they began to accept me. I developed some terrific friendships with them."

Barry's feedback showed substantial change the next year, but not because he had mastered any new technique or skill that he could use in appropriate situations. Barry's feedback changed him because he really cared.

You can fool people for a little while, but most people have the ability to spot a phony. What you change has to become a part of you, or others will perceive that what you are doing is fake. This does not mean you cannot try new things, but ultimately the behavior on the outside has to fit the person on the inside.

8

Making Change Stick

A good friend of mine is an excellent consultant with a very assertive personal style. He can be very bold with clients. For example, he can say to a group of senior executives, "The problem here is that everyone in this room is full of [garbage]," and the client will say, "You're right. We haven't been very explicit about our assumptions; thanks for helping us see the problem."

One of our young associates trained with my friend for several months on a large project. The associate was able to learn by watching the expert in action. Later, the associate tried to use the same approach with a group he was facilitating. But it was an absolute disaster. The people in the group were insulted and disappointed by what he did. What the young man said was essentially the same thing he had observed the senior consultant say, but he could not pull it off in the same way as my friend could. In my opinion, this young associate will never learn this particular skill through practice, no matter how many times he tries.

Similar Ends, Different Means

Luckily, the young associate was astute enough to recognize that he could succeed without having to use the same approach as my friend. After some time, the associate (who was very good with facts and details) developed his own approach to influencing groups. His approach involved presenting the facts in a very organized and logical fashion. He found that he worked best by presenting the facts, and then discussing the implications of those facts. His new approach was much more effective.

Although we must often pass through some radical changes in our personal style, we should never try to become something we are not. Such logic creates problems when the thing we are trying to change is our character or personality. The young associate's goal (to influence groups) did not change. Only his approach to accomplishing the goal changed.

If you are trying to change and it is sucking the life out of you, consider how you have approached the change. Although we all have a range within which we can make adjustments in our behavior, that range is not without realistic limits.

PRINCIPLE 32

Changes that last are those that feel natural and consistent with our core character and personal style.

Our true character and personality is always good and positive, but in attempting to learn from and imitate the style of others, we sometimes lose track of our individuality. Personal greatness comes when people build on the foundation of their core character. Some of us may have forgotten our true core because we have covered it up for so long in trying to assume someone else's style or personality. Think back to your youth, to a time when you were most authentic—that was your genuine style. Think back to a time when you felt good, honest, and true—that was your true character. If you build on these attributes, you will never go wrong.

Creating a Structured Environment

Bill and Jan received the same feedback from the people they manage: "The team needs to have more regularly scheduled meetings." Bill and Jan both accepted the feedback.

Bill began his approach to change by making a firm commitment to meeting more regularly. He took the next step and scheduled the first meeting. After the first meeting, instead of immediately scheduling the next meeting, he decided to wait until there was sufficient need expressed.

Jan, on the other hand, accepted the feedback with less commitment. Since she recognized her own lack of enthusiasm, she decided to schedule all of the meetings for the entire year. Then she shared the dates with her team members and assigned each person on the team to prepare items for an agenda.

By the end of one year, Bill had held six meetings. Every meeting required a great deal of time and effort to schedule, gather information, and conduct. He thought he had made a great deal of improvement, but his team had noticed only a moderate level of improvement.

Jan, on the other hand, ended the year with 24 meetings. She felt that the meetings did not require very much time or effort, and when she asked the team if there had been improvement, the team indicated that there had been significant improvement.

Sometimes significant changes are accomplished by setting up structured conditions and circumstances that lead to the desired change. This structure—whether it involves a day planner, a new organizational structure, or regular up-to-date information—makes change easier to accomplish and longer lasting.

PRINCIPLE 33

Lasting changes often require implementing new systems or structures.

I travel frequently. In the past, I would often forget where I parked my car. I could always find the car, but sometimes it would take as long as 20 minutes. And at the end of a long trip, that can be very frustrating. So, to prevent myself from forgetting, I would try to write down the number of the parking level, and where on that level I had parked, before I went to the airplane. But that was a hassle, and if I was in a hurry, I would sometimes forget to write it down.

Finally, I discovered an area of the parking lot where I knew I could always find a parking place in approximately the same location. Now I always know where my car is parked. I don't have to worry about it, write it down, or even think about it. By simply parking in the same general area every time, I solved my problem. And, although my memory is not any better, I no longer have to focus on remembering, and it always works.

I used to have another problem when I traveled that I also solved with structure. I sometimes forgot to take things such as toothpaste or my razor. This always frustrated me because I would usually not find them missing until very late at night or early the next morning when I really needed them. At first, my solution was to take more time to pack and then check my bag twice. But this required more effort than it was worth, and whenever I was in a hurry I would not have time to do this.

I finally discovered a solution. I acquired a separate toothbrush, toothpaste, razor, brush, and hair dryer for my travel bag. I always keep them in my travel bag, and I never unpack them. This solved my problem, and it saved me time, effort, and worry.

Although not all of the changes we have to make in life can be solved with structure, as humans we tend to consider making personal changes before making structural changes. In my travel examples, my first thoughts about how to solve my memory problems had to do with changing myself: improving my memory, taking more time, checking things twice, writing things down. But, when I applied a simple structure—parking in the same area every time and keeping separate travel toiletries—I no longer felt guilty for short-term memory failure or for not maintaining unrealistic expectations of myself. And I solved the problems.

Finding Strength in Others

Whenever you hear stories of great achievements or personal triumphs, you usually hear about some other significant person who was there to help, such as a coach, spouse, friend, teacher, or boss. Most of these people are either involved naturally (spouse or boss) or contractually (coach or teacher). When we don't have others involved in our change efforts, it is often harder to think of people who can help. An advertisement for such a person might look like this:

> **Wanted:** Someone to provide encouragement, motivation, and inspiration to me while I attempt to make a significant life change. No qualifications necessary, except that I must like and respect you.

Many people find very positive experiences in the role of coach, mentor, or teacher. Some even look for people whom they can coach or teach. If you feel you need a coach, mentor, or teacher, you must initiate the relationship. Ask someone. One person may be too busy; that's all right. Find someone who will help you make changes, who is excited and inspired about the things you are trying to change. This can make a substantial difference in your ability to accomplish your goals.

For example, a high school teacher in California was interested in birds and bird calls. He got his students excited and started a contest. The winners of the contest have appeared on *The Late Show* with David Letterman giving the contest national recognition. Having an inspired coach can make all the difference.

Similarly, I know what a great asset it is to have people around who feel some obligation to "keep me honest." My children do a wonderful job. I once told them I was not going to swear any more. Every time I slipped, they reminded me of my promise.

These kinds of relationships have two different roles. One role is that of the reminder. Sometimes it is hard for us to recognize when we are slipping. Others help us realize when we have returned to our bad habits or have started to rationalize our behavior. The other role is that of moral support. There are certain people in our lives that we never want to disappoint: children, spouses, parents, friends, and business partners. Your goals, when shared with these people, are reinforced by their presence and by the fact that you want to look good in their eyes.

Going the course alone is difficult. The more we internalize our miseries and mistakes, the more likely we are to deceive ourselves about our potential.

Getting others involved may simply mean having a person to run some things past. In college, I had a roommate who once told me about the difficulties he was having with his girlfriend. After he explained the problem, it was clear to me what he should do. I began to tell him my recommendation. His response was, "Will you shut up and listen! I want someone to listen to my problem, not solve it." The solution to the problem was just as clear to him, but he needed to talk about it first.

The Boost of Enthusiasm

Many people find tremendous strength in others without having a one-on-one relationship. For example, by reading the works of a favorite author, many people stay on track and make changes. Others find strength to make change and overcome bad habits by having regular communion with God—God inspires and encourages them to change.

One of my colleagues found his boost of enthusiasm in a very different way. I discovered this one morning when I asked him what he had done the previous night. "I watched TV," he replied.

"What did you watch?" I asked.

"The Weather Channel."

I thought that he must be putting me on—after all, who really watches the weather for entertainment? I continued, "Why did you watch the Weather Channel?"

"Because," he replied, "those people are really enthusiastic, and they like what they do. They get excited about the weather, even on a sunny day."

In getting help from others, keep in mind the following points:

1. Find someone to be your coach or mentor. Use these words: "I have often admired you for your ability to
_____ . Would you consider being my coach

to help me develop these attributes?" Most people will be flattered by the invitation.

2 Make sure you involve people who will not allow you to fail: people who will remind you of your goals, keep you on track, and who you would never want to disappoint. Have them occasionally serve as sounding boards for your new ideas and goals.

3 Find inspiration and motivation for your change. It is much easier to make an inspired change than a boring or mundane one.

Using Technology

We live in a wonderful age in which we have many ways of communicating, keeping ourselves informed, accessing information, and learning. Personal computers, cellular phones, pagers, e-mail, voice mail, audio and videotapes, and video conferencing are all commonplace today. The first step in taking advantage of new technology is to learn how to use it.

PRINCIPLE 34

Increasing your knowledge and skill base, especially in new technologies, will make your efforts to change more effective and increase your self-confidence.

In a recent meeting, some of the participants were discussing their voice-mail system. One person mentioned that the thing he hated most about the system was that if you didn't copy down a phone number quickly, you had to listen to the entire message again to get the phone number.

Someone else responded, "You don't have to listen to the whole message again. You just hit number three, and the system takes you back five seconds in the message."

"Really?" queried the first person. "That's great to know, because I've been replaying my messages for three years!"

Three years of replaying messages represents a great deal of time and frustration. Many new programs require time and practice to learn them and to become proficient in their use. Many people get frustrated because they can't figure out certain programs. When I ask how much time they have spent in trying to learn, usually I find they have spent less than one hour. With any new technology, it takes time to learn, but the rewards can be great for those who learn.

With technology, the learning process often continues for a long time. I had been using a word processing software program for three years, and I thought I knew everything about the program. One day I was sitting next to an employee who worked for the company that developed the word processing program, and I mentioned that the only thing I didn't like about the current version was that I could not split the screen and view two documents at the same time. "Yes you can," he replied, and within a few seconds he had called up two documents at the same time and placed them side-by-side.

Often, the knowledge and experience you acquire on one software program or piece of equipment is transferable to another. Your first software program will likely be the hardest to learn. Then, other programs will usually be easier because they use similar procedures.

Developing New Skills. At first, it seems that some new technologies do not require you to learn any new skills, but, in my experience, it requires many different skills to use new technologies *well*. Frequently, I participate in meetings in which I'll be on a speaker phone or others are connected via speaker phone. Even though I know how to talk on a phone, communicating and influencing others on the phone is very different from doing it in person. Video conferences can also be difficult to manage. Getting everyone to focus on the same piece of information and being able to receive subtle cues from your audience is very different from a typical group setting. Practice is essential in learning how to apply these technologies effectively.

I recently made a presentation to a group in Toronto, while another group tuned in by video conference from New York, and a third group from London. Because I was the one making the presentation, I needed to communicate with all three locations both prior to and during the meeting. But the video technology only allowed us to see one location at a time, and it was voice activated. During the presentation, it was distracting to try to talk and listen to the people in the conference room, while at the same time checking the video screen to gauge the response of only one of the other audiences, and then asking the group not on the screen if they agreed. Many of us have to learn new skills to handle such situations gracefully and effectively.

A few years ago, typing skills were not considered essential for executives. And, although you can still get away without those skills today, your effectiveness will be substantially limited. I recently had a conversation with a senior vice president of a *Fortune* 500 company. His boss, the president, was very adept at typing and sent a lot of e-mail messages. Most people know that the most effective method of responding to an e-mail message is to read the incoming message and then type a reply. But my friend would dictate a message to his secretary and have it typed into the computer. The result was that his replies to the boss's e-mails were always disconnected from the original messages. Further, the process was awkward. Because of his poor typing skills, his ability to respond quickly and fluently was greatly reduced.

In my own experience, I had a difficult time writing in front of a computer screen until I became more comfortable with typing. Having to think about typing while trying to read what was on the screen made it virtually impossible to concentrate on what I was writing. Effective typing skills are becoming an essential skill for everyone.

Making Use of Wasted Time.   Probably one of the greatest advantages of new technologies is that they allow us to make better use of our time. For example, approximately 90 percent of this book was written on airplanes. In the office, things were always too hectic; at home, I became distracted by my children; late at night, I was usually too tired. But, on a plane, I am without phone interruptions and frequently bored. Working on the book was often more entertaining than the movie.

Cellular phones allow car and train travel to be productive time rather than wasted time. Audiotapes in the car can also transform daily commuting from a boring frustration into an educational opportunity.

Tools for Today. Here is a list of some high-tech tools that can help you make your changes stick. I highly recommend them. They are basic to your effectiveness in making lasting change:

- [·] Personal computer
    a. Word processing program
    b. Spreadsheet program
    c. Presentation program
    d. Database program
    e. E-mail and Internet program
- [·] Voice mail
- [·] Cellular phone
- [·] PDA
- [·] E-mail, Internet, or online service

These tools can help you improve in areas such as:

- [·] Communicating regularly
- [·] Keeping others informed
- [·] Staying up-to-date
- [·] Maintaining organization
- [·] Managing time

- Returning calls
- Persuading others
- Preparing effective presentations
- Making effective decisions
- Improving technical competence

Getting Motivated
PRINCIPLE 35

You can only make significant life changes if you have the necessary desire, strength, and motivation to cause those changes to happen.

Change requires energy, strength, and motivation. Often, people want to change, but they lack the strength to make it happen. In order to compete in a marathon you need a combination of strength, endurance, and the motivation or desire to win. When people lack the strength or motivation, the following often can help: removing large distractions, increasing mental strength, getting in shape, maintaining a crystal clear vision of the desired result, describing models for success and failure, focusing on the benefits of change, and planning for success.

Remove Large Distractions. At times, all of us have significant distractions that seem to diminish our strength and motivation. Sometimes we cause these distractions ourselves (perhaps an argument with a friend or family member). Other times, distractions are caused by others or by circumstances (divorce, sickness, or death of a loved one). Trying to make changes happen during such distractions is almost always impossible. There is very little energy or motivation left.

Sometimes these distractions, in and of themselves, can cause us to lose all sense of priority. Two examples of what I mean follow.

Tom was going through a divorce. In the months following his separation, his performance on the job declined significantly. Because of his anger and frustration—as well as his desire to have the terms of the divorce not favor his wife—he dragged the process out as long as he could. Through all of this, Tom's performance at work continued to decline. His boss approached him and, in a straightforward manner, pointed out the poor performance. Tom acknowledged his lack of effort and told his boss he would improve.

Tom focused his efforts on trying to change, but the improvements were small. It wasn't until several months after the divorce had been finalized that Tom began to make moderate improvements. And his performance did not begin to change noticeably until he was able to resolve the divorce emotionally. Paradoxically, the money he was able to keep by dragging out the divorce process was small compared to the bonus dollars he forfeited due to his poor performance.

Amy was upset. A friend of hers had helped her select some computer equipment, but the printer she purchased would not work with the new computer. She complained, "He should have known that the printer wouldn't work with that machine. I can't believe he did that to me. Now what will I do?"

The facilitator suggested it might be a simple problem—anybody could have made the same mistake—and she could trade the printer in for a printer that was compatible.

"Well, it's not that simple," she continued. "I know I will lose money by doing it that way. He needs to make up the difference; he should have known better!"

By the time Amy had finished assigning blame and demanding compensation, she had consumed an entire month in resolving the problem. She forced her friend to pay the difference, which amounted to less than $50, but her action promptly ended their friendship. She had been so obsessed with the dilemma that her performance at work had suffered, and her stress level became incredibly high.

All of us have experienced traumatic emotional events that have caused us to be distracted. In such situations, we must focus our energy on getting through the emotional event as our first priority. Too frequently, rather than resolve the emotional event, we drag it out, possibly hoping to gain more by doing so.

In these examples, Tom missed out on financial bonuses and a possible promotion by bringing his family life into the office. Amy took a month to solve a problem that could have been solved in an hour. Dragging out problems may help you win the battle, only to lose the war.

Additionally, the cost of emotional distress is high. Whenever we try to handle significant distractions, while at the same time maintaining the same or increasing levels of performance, productivity almost always declines. Stress begins to exert both physical and psychological pressure. Some people can work through emotional events with relative ease and speed, while others seem to hang on to the events forever. The difference in speed likely has something to do with your perspective. For example, if you believe that grieving over the death of a loved one for a long time is the most effective way for you to demonstrate your commitment for that loved one, then you will probably grieve for a long time. However, if you believe that a brief period of grief, followed by a quick return to normal activity, is what a loved one would have wanted you to do, then your period of grief might be shorter.

In Amy's case, the facilitator asked her why she had felt so compelled to pursue the issue, and why she didn't just go out and solve the problem. She remarked, "My friend needed to learn a lesson. He needs to learn how to be responsible for his actions, and I was trying to teach him what is right." But, in the end, she was just frustrated. Her friend hadn't learned a thing, except that he no longer wanted to be her friend.

I understand that some issues are worth pursuing—worth many times the distress, frustration, sleepless nights, depression, and tears that may be invested. But the majority of disagreements I see between people fall into the trivial category.

Increase Internal Mental Strength. For people trying to make significant changes in their lives, I recommend that you regularly listen to tapes and read books on motivation, change, and personal improvement. By teaching and training yourself in terms of "I can," you will find that it is true.

Ben had received some harsh feedback, but he sounded motivated to make a change. I was concerned that he might not stick to such a rigorous plan for change. I told him I would send him a set of motivational tapes on change, and I asked him to promise me that he would listen to the tapes every day for a month. His initial reaction was, "Only wimps use that stuff." But I asked him to humor me and do it anyway. He agreed.

I met with Ben six weeks later. He had made great progress. I asked him what had been the most helpful. "Those tapes," he said. "I listened to them every morning on the way to work. They really kept me going."

Get in Shape. It is easier for me to change when I feel good and have plenty of physical energy. When I am in shape I feel stronger and have more energy—not just physical energy, but mental energy and focus. I strongly recommend that you:

- ☐ Get into and stay in excellent physical condition.
- ☐ Exercise often. Regular exercise provides additional physical and mental energy.
- ☐ Improve your diet. Eating healthy foods can substantially improve your energy.
- ☐ Learn to relax, meditate, and concentrate. This is a great skill that is absolutely essential for managing stress.

Have a Crystal Clear Vision. Those who change successfully have either formed a crystal clear vision of what they want to do or become, or they have accidentally fallen into change by luck or fate. Those who are unsuccessful only have a vague picture that is always murky, never crystal clear. In their attempts to change, the picture often becomes more and more abstract and generalized. Finally, after some time, they begin to believe that they have achieved their goal, when in reality all they did was modify their goal to fit current reality.

Clear vision is absolutely essential to success. One of the most effective ways to clarify your vision is not only to describe what you want, but also to do the opposite: Describe what you don't want. We can often gain greater clarity by focusing on what our vision is not, which helps us to clarify what our vision is.

If you are not currently crystal clear about your plans for change, don't worry. Most people begin with only a vague notion of what they want to change. A vision is most often clarified over time. The clarification process can be facilitated by several helpful factors. To describe your vision and plans for change, start with a blank piece of paper. Then ask yourself the following questions related to what your vision is:

- ☑ What do I want to change (generally speaking)?
- ☑ Who do I know that does this well?
- ☑ Who do I know that does this poorly?

- What is the biggest difference between those who are successful and those who are unsuccessful with this skill?
- If I were another person looking at myself doing this well, what would I look like?
- What do I think about when I perform this skill best?
- How do I feel when I perform well?

Sometimes it is easier to describe what you do not want than what you want. Ask yourself the following questions related to what your vision is not:

- What are the things I do not want to happen (generally speaking)?
- What would the worst example of not performing this skill look like?
- What behaviors come close to the change, but are not what I want?

Describe a Model for Success and Failure. Models help us understand the world. They often include descriptions of both success and failure, as well as the many stages of a process under a variety of conditions.

Shirley received feedback about the amount of work she had back-logged but never got around to doing. Many important projects had been held up because they had been on her desk for over a month before she had even looked at them.

Her boss encouraged her to delegate more of her work to others in the company. He also warned her about sharing proprietary knowledge with too many people, since he feared other employees might quit and start their own companies, replicating the technology.

After receiving this feedback, Shirley listed all of the projects she was working on. She first tried to prioritize the projects, but found it too difficult to assign priorities. She then constructed a model to describe the various projects.

She reasoned that two kinds of work were assigned to her: *strategic* (work that created competitive advantage for the business) and *business essential* (work that needed to be done but did not add value to the company). She also reasoned that each kind of work was divided into two types: *generic* (common knowledge) and *proprietary* (trade secrets). Shirley laid out the model in a simple diagram (see Figure 8.1).

After developing the model, Shirley was quickly able to classify her work according to the model. She shared the results with her boss. Several projects were delegated to

	Proprietary	Generic
Strategic	Top Priority Do Myself	Second Priority Delegate within Work Group
Business Essential	Third Priority Delegate within the Company	Fourth Priority Outsource

Figure 8.1   Shirley's prioritization model.

employees in the company, and others were given to outside vendors. As new requests for her time came in, Shirley used the model to decide how the work could be completed.

Keep the Vision in Mind. A clear vision is thought about and considered frequently. Thinking about something frequently helps to keep it in focus. When I was 16, my uncle (who I was working for) once made my day by allowing me to plow his field with a big Caterpillar tractor. This was great fun, and it didn't seem too difficult. My uncle sat next to me for the first round. I thought I had been doing a pretty good job. But, when I got to the end of the row, he told me to look back. When I looked, I noticed how wavy my furrow looked compared to his. "Your problem," he told me, "is that you are looking at the ground right in front of the tractor. Focus your attention on that fence post at the other end of the field, and you will plow straight." That was great advice. It taught me to plow straight. It also taught me a lot about life. Visions have to be kept in mind and focused on constantly in order to have impact.

Remember the Benefits. Part of your clear vision should include some idea of the benefits associated with making a change. Making the benefits clear helps you remember why you are willing to work so hard to make this change. Too often, we become clear about the liabilities associated with change. We only focus on the negative consequences of change, and forget about the benefits. Focusing on negative consequences is never as motivating as focusing on positive ones.

Consider the problem of spouse abuse. If a person is abusive but is trying to change, a negative motivation might be trying to avoid being put in jail and fined. Such a motivation only solves the problem in the short term, and perhaps not even at all. But, if the person focuses on the benefits of the new behavior, such as forming a positive, loving relationship with a spouse, and gaining the trust and confidence of others, the change will more likely stick. A clear focus on the benefits of change can be very helpful in forming a clear vision.

Follow Up. At the end of training or coaching sessions, most of the people I meet with are sincerely committed to make a change. They have an action plan; they feel committed and want to change. It is always interesting to call people up a month after the session and ask them how they are doing. Some report that they are still on track and making progress, but others say things like, "Oh yes, that goal. Well, things have been very busy, and I . . ." Everyone knows the importance of being reminded of their commitments.

It is interesting how much most people hate to be reminded of their commitments. It's as if we believe that if we are not reminded, we are not responsible. I recently received a phone call reminding me of an early morning meeting the next day. The meeting was informational but not critical, but I had agreed to attend. After taking the call, I thought to myself about how much I wished I had not received the reminder phone call. I had completely forgotten about the meeting. If the reminder call had not come, I would not have attended. And I wouldn't have felt guilty either, because I had put it completely out of my mind. Not remembering allowed me to have a reasonable excuse.

I recently reviewed some research on the effects of follow-up on goal attainment. The data is incontrovertible about the impact of follow-up. The likelihood of change doubles if people establish a regular process of reminding themselves of their commitments. The reminders do not need to be harsh or judgmental. If you set up a regular process that reminds you of your commitments, you will be twice as likely to achieve those commitments.

A vice president of executive development in a large *Fortune 500* company got excited about using a formal follow-up system to assist managers in achieving their change goals. The follow-up system was presented to the top management group. Each member of the group was very enthusiastic about using the process for managers throughout the organization. Each of them could think of specific examples of managers who had failed to change because their leader had not followed up on a developmental opportunity. Hearing their enthusiasm, the vice president of executive development took a rather bold position and said, "If you believe this follow-up system is necessary for managers, then I assume that all of you here would want to use this for yourself." The room went silent.

Finally, one executive spoke up, "I don't think we need this kind of hand holding. We are beyond this."

My experience is that no one is "beyond this," but almost everyone loves to avoid the accountability that comes with follow-up.

Plan to Win. Most people plan to play, but only a few plan how they will win. Planning to win doesn't mean just making a plan. Some plans never allow us to win; they are just plans. Most seem reasonable, logical, and understandable, but very few strike me as compelling. They provide a reasonable approach, but they lack energy, motivation, and force. A plan to win is a serious attempt at setting forth a strategy that has high probability of success. Ask yourself the following questions about your change plan:

- ☐ If you had to face a firing squad if you didn't make this change, how would your plan be different?
- ☐ If all of your success in life were contingent on you making this change, how would your plan be different?
- ☐ Does your plan take advantage of all the resources under your control?
- ☐ Is the plan modest or aggressive?
- ☐ What could you do to your plan to take it to the next level, or even higher?

Don't confuse having a winning game plan with being overly competitive. With change, your major source of competition is always yourself. Can you push yourself to a higher level? Can you motivate yourself to go for more? Are you willing to challenge yourself to do more than you thought possible? You can do all these things if you are willing, if you want to, and if you try. The key to turning feedback into change is within you. The techniques, models, theories, and philosophies can all help, but you and your desire to change are key.

9

Working Harder or Working Smarter?

Several years ago, I worked with a large government contractor. My contact, a former navy officer, was mentoring me in my work. He told me, "You're pretty good at what you do, but I am going to make you great." Each time I visited the client, he would give me tips and hints on how to improve. Even though I sincerely tried to implement his suggestions, none of them seemed to have any profound impact. The experience left me wondering what had gone wrong. Sometimes the direct, head-on approach does not result in change.

In Chapter 3, I presented some of the findings that Jack Zenger and I uncovered in our analysis of successful people. We found that those who were most successful at accepting feedback were also skillful in several related areas, called *companion behaviors*. Now I would like to share with you what we found about people who were successful in actually making changes.[1] We found a similar list of companion behaviors when we analyzed the people who'd had the most success in making changes. These companion behaviors will allow you to take an indirect, and perhaps more helpful, approach to change. Since what creates exceptional ability is the interaction of multiple skills, becoming proficient in one or more of these companion skills will allow you to make more progress than if you were to exhaust yourself using the head-on approach.

In our research we also found that, although the process of going from poor performance to good performance is often straightforward and intuitive, a much less intuitive approach is needed to move from good or average to great. It is usually very clear what needs to be done to improve poor performance. Weakness, errors, or problems are clear to see, and the solutions are often intuitively obvious. But the process of going from good to great is much less obvious and often requires improvement in these companion skills.

A high level of personal effectiveness requires three things: First, you cannot have any *fatal flaws.* A fatal flaw is a behavior that has an overpoweringly negative impact on your overall perceived effectiveness. A fatal flaw will hold any person back from achieving his or her potential. If you have a fatal flaw, you have to fix it. This doesn't mean you have to make it into a profound strength, but you have to improve to the point where it is no longer a negative issue for you. Second, you need to have a few strengths. To be effective, we all must have skills that will be valued in some way by the organization. Since organizations value many things, you can choose, to a large extent, what you would like to do well. Third, being good at something is very different from being great. Too often, people become satisfied with adequate performance. Adequate performance is not the same as having a strength. Remember, we defined a strength as a core competency rated at the 90th percentile or higher.

Companion Behaviors for Change

To gather insights on a nonlinear approach to personal change, we compiled a data set from thousands of people who had been engaged in a change process. We looked at individuals who were viewed as effective at making personal changes and looked for companion behaviors. We found that people who were most effective at making change were also competent at eight companion skills. Improvement in the companion skills may improve an individual's ability to make a change. Jack Zenger and I called this approach *nonlinear development* because the companion skills are sometimes counterintuitive. The eight companion skills are:

1. Passion and willingness to make a difference
2. Accepts feedback
3. Trust
4. Shows concern and consideration for others
5. Innovation
6. Develops others
7. Optimism
8. Establishes clear goals and priorities

Passion and Willingness to Make a Difference.
Think again about something big you have been able to change in your life (e.g., quitting smoking, losing weight, getting out of a bad relationship). Were you able to make this change in your life without passion, energy, or commitment? Unless the change is easy, people are rarely able to change unless they are passionate and committed.

Recently, I was working with a group in Silicon Valley. We were discussing some research that indicated child prodigies achieved their great skills and talent because of years of practice. I told a story about a young child who had a great desire to play the piano. The child approached his parents and said, "I want to play the piano." The parents responded by signing the child up for lessons. At first, the child did not seem to be very talented. But by practicing every day for several years, his talent emerged.

After hearing the story, a man in the back of the room raised his hand and said, "That stuff about practice is not true."

I asked the man what he meant. He said, "My mother made me take piano lessons for five years, and I still can't play a note."

I was well prepared to respond, because my mother made me take piano lessons, also, and I can't play a note either. I asked the man, "What was the difference between you and the example I described."

He thought for a moment and then said, "That child wanted to play the piano."

Occasionally, as I work with clients reviewing their feedback data, they ask me, "As the expert, what do you think I should change?"

My response is always the same: I ask, "What do you want to change?" It doesn't really matter if I feel an issue is important because, in my experience, people change the things they care about changing. It would be impossible to make a difficult change if the person wasn't passionate about making the change. I call this lack of passion the "good soldier" syndrome. You do what you are supposed to do when you are supposed to do it, but you do it out of duty, not passion, desire, or excitement. Having passion, being excited, and believing in what you are doing make a huge difference in being totally successful.

As people work in their jobs over a period of time, they tend to settle in. Rather than looking for opportunities to learn, grow, and develop, they look forward to performing at the same pace they have worked at in the past and leveraging their existing skills. They look at new challenges as chores or burdens. It is impossible to help people to change when they resist doing additional work. Perceiving change as a chore causes people to feel like the change is just another "to do" on a list that is already far too long. But viewing change as an exciting learning experience makes people feel very differently about their efforts to improve.

What can you do if you feel you lack the passion needed to succeed in making a change?

First, focus your efforts for change in areas where you have some passion. Often, we are told what thing we "ought" to improve, but the reality is that nothing will change if we act out of duty and obligation.

Second, keep focused on the goal. Many times, we focus too much attention on activities, and not enough on the goal. How do you feel when you accomplish something significant? How do you feel when you are successful? Focusing on the goal helps people find their passion again.

Third, don't procrastinate. Many people don't enjoy certain tasks. Jump in and get them done quickly, so you can focus on the fun stuff. Procrastination creates a burden. It is like dragging around a ball and chain.

Accepts Feedback.   In this book, we have already spent several chapters discussing the importance of accepting feedback. It is difficult to understand why people resist accepting feedback when it can be such a benefit to them.

Prior to working on this chapter, I was driving with my wife to the store. I pulled out in front of another car on a major street. She shouted, "Watch out!"

I said, "Don't worry, I'm fine. Relax, I knew the car was coming."

She responded, "Better go back and work some more on your feedback book."

Although feedback is there to help us, the reality is that accepting the feedback we receive is a difficult skill to master.

Trust.   People who are trusted are also more effective at making personal change. Trusted people can be counted on to keep commitments. They walk their talk and set good examples. To understand how being trusted helps people to change, consider a situation in which a person who is attempting to change is not trusted. The person's motives are constantly questioned: "What is he really trying to do?" "Is this just for show?" "Is she really serious?" Although it is possible for people to make changes on their own, without help from others, it is clear that when others involved are coaching and supportive the change is much more likely to occur.

In our research, when we interviewed people with exceptional skills, we asked them how they were able to develop their skills. The most typical answer was, "I was given a job assignment that forced me to learn this skill." As a person attempts to change, a new assignment can be a critical part of making the change permanent. It requires some risk. If there is little trust between a manager and an employee, the likelihood of a getting a new assignment is very low.

Change requires risk taking. Imagine an environment in which you don't trust others and they don't trust you. In that kind of environment, most people would be unwilling to take risks, because they would be afraid of what might happen if they failed. Building strong, trusting relationships creates the kind of environment where people are more willing to take risks.

Marshall Goldsmith is a nationally recognized executive coach. He works with executives on helping them to change. One of the first things he does with new clients is ask them to go to their direct reports, peers, and boss

Working Harder or Working Smarter?

and apologize for past behavior. He considers this step to be a critical part of the change effort, because when others don't trust you, they won't allow you to change. Apologizing to others gets them helping with the change instead of criticizing the change effort. However, although apologies begin the process of building trust, they must be followed by action.

Shows Concern and Consideration for Others. Those who showed a high level of concern and consideration for others are more likely to make personal changes. If a person doesn't care about others, what is the motivation to change? If we don't value other people, then we will not value the opinions or feedback of others. Some people find it difficult to show consideration for others, because they feel they lack the ability to please most of the people most of the time. It seems that someone is always offended, discontent, or critical no matter what effort is made. Such people begin to assume that, since they can't please everyone, they might as well please themselves.

Those who have little concern or consideration for others face making changes by themselves, with little help or assistance from others. This is the best-case scenario for them, because showing little concern for others often alienates others so much that they begin to work against any change efforts. Those who do help tend to do so out of duty, not out of concern.

One senior manager demonstrated such a disconnection from others when he said, "I don't want to get too close to any of my people, because I may need to fire them." This manager maintained what he saw as a reasonable distance between himself and his direct reports. In turn, they also maintained their distance. Consequently, change efforts on both sides were viewed with suspicion. Yet, a substantial body of research shows that getting others to help in making a change substantially improves the chances that the change efforts will be successful.

Realistically, if people only changed those things that would personally benefit them, the list of changes that would be made would be very short. Most of the changes people make are for the benefit of others. The reality of life is that, when we help other people, other people are more likely to help us. When we are concerned about other people, other people are more concerned about us. And, when we are considerate of others' circumstances, they become considerate of ours. So, unless you have an organization of one, with no customers, you need other people to be on your side when you attempt to make a change.

Sometimes, people are not so concerned about others, because they are totally focused on their own problems. Many people face tragic circumstances, including emotional misery or physical pain, every day. Perhaps they feel they have a good reason to have an internal rather than an external focus. But my experience in life has taught me that, in most cases, the best way for me to solve my internal problems is to focus on helping other people solve their problems. The effect is almost miraculous.

Innovation. Innovative people are more effective at making personal changes. Although it is possible to "grind out" a change, finding new and creative approaches to keep the change process alive makes the possibility of change much more likely.

Over time, change can become a chore. It is sometimes difficult to see past all the work that needs to be done. The work looks like hard labor. As you begin a change effort, ask yourself what would make the effort fun. Think of ways to approach the change that are new and exciting. Ask others for ideas on different ways of making the change. The most frequent mistake people make in trying to change is that they fail to involve others and ask for their ideas, help, and assistance. To improve your innovative approach to change, ask 10 people for their ideas on how to go about changing a specific behavior. Inevitably, you will hear at least one new and helpful idea you never would have considered.

Develops Others. Those who are interested in helping others change and improve their skills are more likely to improve their own skills. Those who help others to develop learn from the experience. They can then apply what they have learned to their own development. This is an excellent example of how service to others benefits the person who serves.

Optimism. Change is hard enough as it is. Imagine how difficult it would be if you believed that no matter what you did, you could never be successful. People who are optimistic are willing to attempt change because they assume their change efforts will be successful. Even if they fall short, they believe they will benefit in some way. However, pessimists assume that their efforts will be futile and will only create frustration.

Optimism generates many other benefits, as well. For example, optimists tend to live longer, have better overall health, make more money, and have better relationships. Viktor Frankl, in his book, *Man's Search for Meaning,* describes his experience in a Nazi concentration camp.[2] In the concentration camp, almost everything was taken away from him. His family was killed; he was starved, cold, and treated inhumanly every day. With so much misery and loss, how could he find life worth living? What Frankl found was that he had control over one essential thing: his attitude. He could choose to hope. He also observed was those who lost hope died the fastest.

Some people approach the feedback and change processes with anger. They are angry about having to change and blame other people or their circumstances. But people choose anger. It is also possible for them to choose to be enthusiastic about the opportunity to improve themselves. They could be grateful that others care enough about them to give them feedback. They can choose to believe that, if they work hard, they will be successful.

Establishes Clear Goals and Priorities. Those who are effective at establishing clear goals and priorities are also more effective at making personal changes. To change, a person needs a clear plan and specific priorities. After all, you will not be able to change everything. Change often starts as a grand idea, but if the idea does not become a clear, actionable goal then the change will never last. Clear goals need to be written down.

It is always amazing what happens when I force myself to write down good ideas. In my mind, the idea begins so clear. But as I write it down, I recognize my lack of clarity. Writing down a goal provides an excellent way to organize, store, and remind us of our good intentions.

Improving Your Ability to Change

These eight companion behaviors provide a nonlinear approach to change. As you review the companion behaviors, identify one or two areas where you see an opportunity to improve. You don't necessarily need to improve companion behaviors where your skills are the lowest. Improvement in any of these skills will help you increase your ability to create personal change. Often, as people read through the companion behaviors, they will see one that in some ways solves the mystery of "Why haven't I been able to change?" In reading through the content, people often find a connection that they had not seen before. For example, "I have never made personal development a priority. Achieving organizational goals has always been my priority, and that has always taken precedence over my individual development."

Recently, several popular books have suggested that a person's behavior is either driven by genetics or fixed in place at a young age. The result of such logic is the idea that people can't change—that they are fixed in their places by factors beyond their control. The advice from such logic is just to continue to do what you do well and forget about the rest because if you don't have a talent for something when you are 16, you're never going to develop that talent. This pessimistic philosophy discourages people from even trying to change, believing that the world must simply accept them the way they are. The philosophy can also create an entitlement mentality, in which people assume that organizations have the obligation to find them an appropriate job where they can utilize their talents. This philosophy negatively impacts both individuals and organizations. For individuals, it discourages them from even trying to develop new skills and talents. And it makes organizations responsible for every individual's job satisfaction.

I have spent the past 30 years providing feedback to people and helping them make changes. I have measured the improvements they have made. I know that people can change. Most personal changes are not instantaneous or immediate. They all require practice and commitment. If you want to learn a new sport, you would expect that practice would be involved. The first time a person plays golf, they often find it frustrating. But, over time and with practice, they become better. Making up your mind to change a behavior and then creating an action plan does not, in and of itself, create change. But, in my experience, the more you practice the better you get. People must also realize that practice is different from performance. To practice, people must evaluate their

Working Harder or Working Smarter?

performance and look for ways to improve. Just doing something over and over is not practice unless some feedback and evaluation is provided and further attempts are made to improve accept and integrate that feedback.

Last summer, I accompanied my son on a backpacking expedition in which we climbed to an altitude of 10,000 feet. As I looked at myself in the mirror one month before the hike, I thought of a man I had known, about my age, who'd had a heart attack on a hike with his son and died. The father-son bonding experience turned into a tragedy that permanently scarred the son. That thought gave me a feeling of fear that motivated me to take action. I immediately began that week to ride my bike, take short hikes and walks, and begin watching my diet a bit better. I had taken something that I had neglected, which I knew I ought to be doing, and I made it into a clear priority for myself. This was a critical step in starting the change.

I have a long list of things I ought to be doing, and exercise has always been on that list. But, as I reflected on the man I had known, I felt that health was now a priority I could not afford to leave at the bottom of my list. Because I was motivated by fear, the exercise routine seemed difficult. Every bike ride left me stiff, and on every practice hike I discovered a new ache. As the hike approached, I began to feel minimally prepared. But upon donning my 30-pound backpack at the beginning of the trail (altitude 8,800 feet), I realized it was going to be a very long hike.

I was able to move along fairly well on the hike. But having done this same hike five years before, I soon realized how out of shape I really was. Returning home, I felt I ought to continue to exercise. But the initial motivation that had driven me to increase my level exercise (my fear of dying) had now passed. I needed a new motivation.

Doing an activity just because you are supposed to, because it is good for you, only takes you so far. Any reasonable excuse will allow you to blow off your routine for another day. As long as I saw exercise as a chore, it would never become a permanent habit. However, since I had survived the many aches and pains of the first month of exercise, and since the hike had left me in reasonable shape, I started to feel different about exercising. I found it to be a valuable release from the stresses of an intense day at work. I discovered the challenge of beating my time and going farther. I found I was much better able to present an eight-hour training session and maintain a high level of energy.

Along the way, I lost some weight and my blood pressure came down. But, more important, in doing the exercises I experienced joy. It is not always joyful, especially when I begin my exercise each day. But, as I settle into the routine, I enjoy the experience, and, when I can't exercise, I miss the experience. I find myself looking forward to exercising. I see that I have a passion for it. It isn't difficult to continue something you have passion for, but the passion and joy don't come until you work through the initial phase of aches and pains.

My experience with making this change is fairly typical. The beginning is always difficult. It requires plenty of motivation and persistence. The companion behavior that helped me begin was making exercise a priority. I did not experience much joy at first, only hard work and pain. In most change efforts, our first tries will be difficult or even embarrassing. We want to improve quickly, but most changes take time and continued effort. Over time, in order for change to continue, we need to find joy or passion in the new thing we are doing—note that I said "find" joy or passion. Usually, the joy does not find you; the passion is an acquired taste, and both are things you need to find along the way. Sometimes you find joy and passion in doing something better; sometimes they are found in persistence, or in the responses of others. But joy and passion are both necessary to continue improving a new behavior.

Even though we may find passion and joy in our change efforts, many aspects will continue to be difficult and painful. After having written six books, many people have commented to me, "You must love to write." Well, I love to complete the task of writing, and I love seeing the finished product. But the process of getting there requires a lot of work and is very challenging. These books never get written unless I make some changes in my daily priorities. The passion comes from doing something that may make a difference in the lives of other people.

I do not personally believe that anybody can become great at everything they do, but I am convinced that every person can become very proficient in a few unique things. In many ways, each one of us must discover our own genius. We need to figure out what we can do to make a contribution to the world. I hope these examples provide you with a better sense of how you can use companion behaviors to help you in making a change. Some companion behaviors seem to help more than others, depending on what you are trying to change. Think of these companion behaviors as another lever that assists you in lifting yourself to a new level of performance.

Afterword

There are no overnight transformations. Often, people attend training events and come back expecting to be automatically "fixed." My experience is that change occurs only through sustained effort over time. Most people are not optimistic about the extent to which change occurs in others. When asked how often they see significant changes in others, most people say, "Rarely." Change is often hard to see. But when we ask people how often they see long-term growth in others, they say, "Frequently."

When I go on a trip for a week and come home, my children always seem to look different. They have changed in ways that I probably wouldn't have noticed had I been with them all week. Most change occurs slowly and subtlety over time.

We tend to accept and be satisfied with our current circumstances. Otherwise, we would feel that we are failing in our attempts to change, which leads to the perception that we are failing as individuals. We assume our failures are well disguised and that they are not common knowledge, but almost everyone who knows us well is acquainted with our failures. Our successes are not as easily recognized. For this reason, receiving feedback can be difficult.

I do not recommend foolhardy experimentation in attempting change, but instead consistent, calculated efforts to improve. None of us has "arrived." New and different challenges face us every day. Even the process of aging creates situations that make change necessary to maintain our effectiveness.

The risks of changing will always be highest when you attempt it alone. Involving others in change efforts not only improves the odds of change, but it also provides motivation for improvement.

People can discover a better life when they make a contribution to the world. When you are making a contribution, you feel valued and other people value you. You feel a sense of worth for having done something well and not having any fatal flaws. If you can't make a contribution in your current situation, then either you need to change yourself or you need to change your situation. Choosing to put up with a bad situation will also change you. But it will make you tired, cynical, pessimistic, and depressed. I hope you don't make that choice.

You have the capacity to receive feedback, accept feedback, and make positive change. No person can force you to change, and no one can change for you. To change, you have to try. If you try you might fail, but you can learn from failure and eventually produce the desired result and turn your feedback into change.

Notes

CHAPTER 1: Reacting to Feedback

1. Ronald J. Comer, *Abnormal Psychology,* New York: W. H. Freeman and Company, 1996.

CHAPTER 2: Why Did I Get That Feedback?

1. Solomon E. Asch, "Forming Impressions of Personality," *Journal of Abnormal and Social Psychology,* vol. 41 (1946), 258–290.

2. Charles A. Dailey, "The Effects of Premature Conclusions upon the Acquisition of Understanding of a Person," *Journal of Psychology,* vol. 33 (1952), 133–152.

3. Alvin Scodel and Paul Mussen, "Social Perceptions of Authoritarians and Nonauthoritarians," *Journal of Abnormal and Social Psychology,* vol. 48 (1953), 181–184.

4. Harold H. Kelley, "The Process of Casual Attribution," *American Psychologist,* vol. 28 (1973), 107–128.

5. Camille B. Wortman, "Causal Attributions and Personal Control," in *New Direction in Attribution Research, Vol. 1,* John H. Harvey, William John Ickes, and Robert F. Kidd, eds., Hillsdale, NJ: Lawrence Erlbaum Associates, 1976.

6. Melvin J. Lerner, "The Desire for Justice and Reactions to Victims," in *Altruism and Helping Behavior: Social Psychological Studies of Some Antecedents and Consequences,* Jacqueline R. Macaulay and Leonard Berkowitz, eds., New York: Academic Press, 1970.

CHAPTER 3: Improving Your Ability to Accept Feedback

1. The original research on the companion behaviors of receiving feedback in this chapter first appeared in John F. Zenger, and Joe Folkman, *The Extraordinary Leader,* New York: McGraw-Hill, 2002.

2. Gene W. Dalton, Louis B. Barnes, and Abraham Zaleznik, *The Distribution of Authority in Formal Organizations,* Boston: MIT Press, 1973.

CHAPTER 4: Why Change?

1. Walter Cannon, *The Wisdom of the Body,* New York: W. W. Norton & Company, 1932.

CHAPTER 5: Deciding What to Change

1. Gene W. Dalton, Louis B. Barnes, and Abraham Zaleznik, *The Distribution of Authority in Formal Organizations,* Boston: MIT Press, 1973.

CHAPTER 6: Fixing Weaknesses or Building Strengths?

1. The original research on the impact of strengths in this chapter first appeared in John F. Zenger, and Joe Folkman, *The Extraordinary Leader,* New York: McGraw-Hill, 2002.

CHAPTER 7: Making Change Happen

1. Gene W. Dalton, Louis B. Barnes, and Abraham Zaleznik, *The Distribution of Authority in Formal Organizations,* Boston: MIT Press, 1973.

2. Solomon E. Asch, *Social Psychology,* New York: Prentice Hall, 1952.

3. See note 1.

4. W. Timothy Gallwey, *The Inner Game of Tennis,* New York: Random House, 1974.

5. Carole Hyatt and Linda Gottlieb, *When Smart People Fail: Rebuilding Yourself for Success,* New York: Penguin, 1987.

6. Matthew McKay and Patrick Fanning, *Prisoners of Belief: Exposing & Changing Beliefs That Control Your Life,* Oakland, CA: New Harbinger, 1991.

7. See note 1.

CHAPTER 9: Working Harder or Working Smarter?

1. The original research on the companion behaviors for making change in this chapter first appeared in John F. Zenger, and Joe Folkman, *The Extraordinary Leader,* New York: McGraw-Hill, 2002.

2. Viktor Frankl, *Man's Search for Meaning, rev. and updated ed.,* New York: Washington Square Press, 1984.

Index

199

Index

About the Author

Joseph Folkman is president of Zenger | Folkman, a firm that is focused on assisting individuals and organizations to create exceptional performance. Joseph Folkman and his partner, Jack Zenger, have created workshops, assessments, and a follow-up process that have been adopted by *Fortune* 500 companies around the world. Folkman has over 30 years of experience in teaching and coaching leaders, survey research and analysis, and consulting in areas of organizational diagnosis and leadership assessment. A founding partner of Novations Group, Inc., Folkman received his doctorate in organizational psychology and his master's degree in organizational behavior from Brigham Young University. His research has been published in the *Wall Street Journal's National Business Employment Weekly, Personnel,* and *Executive Excellence.*

Folkman has consulted with some of the world's most prestigious and successful organizations—both large and small, both public and private. The diversity of clients has provided a powerful learning opportunity and an exceptional research base. He has spent most of his career finding better ways to measure individual and organizational effectiveness, and then using that data to help people create change. He is a frequent keynote speaker and conference presenter on a variety of topics regarding leadership, feedback, and individual and organizational change. He is the author or coauthor of five previous books: *Turning Feedback into Change, Making Feedback Work, Employee Surveys That Make a Difference, The Extraordinary Leader,* and *Handbook for Leaders.*

He lives in Orem, Utah, with his wife, Laura, and their five children: Brandon, Rachel, BreAnne, Matthew, and Corbin.

For more information on products and programs from Joseph Folkman, contact:

Zenger | Folkman Co., Inc.
610 E. Technology Ave., Bldg. B, Ste. 2100
Orem, UT 84097
(801) 705-9490
Fax (801) 705-9376
www.zfco.com